Antique Embossing™

BASIC MATERIALS: Mini Matts™ shapes • Ivory acrylic paint • Pin back • Heat tool • Paintbrush • 1/8" hole punch • Chalk • FabriTac • Terry cloth

1. Stamp design with Clear ink, then sprinkle with Clear embossing powder.

2. Melt powder with heat tool to emboss image.

3. Apply the acrylic paint and let dry.

4. Gently scrub paint from embossed areas using damp terry cloth.

5. Rub with chalk and punch hole. Embellish as desired.

6. Outline the edges with metallic marker.

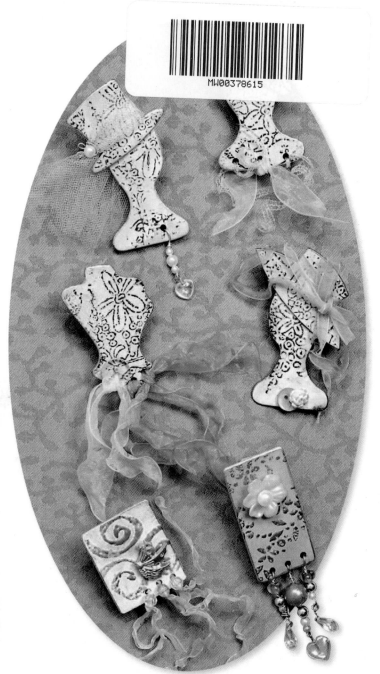

Pink Lady - MATERIALS: Black Millinery Mini Matts • Millefiori Vase rubber stamp • Clear embossing ink • Deep Impression Clear embossing powder • Ivory acrylic paint • 22 gauge Silver wire • Pink tulle circle • Ivory pearl beads • Small Pink pearl beads • Translucent heart charm • Round-nose pliers • Metallic Silver marker • Pink chalk
TIPS: Attach beads and heart charm with Silver wire. Wrap tulle around hat and secure with wire and pearl bead. Attach hat to head and pin back to finished piece.

Elegance in Ivory - MATERIALS: Black Millinery Mini Matts • Millefiori Bouquet rubber stamp • Clear embossing ink • Deep Impression Clear embossing powder • Ivory acrylic paint • Crystal flower and Gold bead • Iridescent 1/4" twist and 3/4" Lemon sheer ribbon • 22 gauge Silver wire • Round-nose pliers • Metallic Gold marker • White and Yellow chalk
TIPS: Punch 3 holes in base. Tie twist ribbon through 2 holes. Tie Yellow ribbon through hole in center. Punch 2 holes in hat. Insert and attach beads with wire, curling ends. Attach hat to head and pin back to finished piece.

Beribboned Torso - MATERIALS: Black Millinery Mini Matts Torso • Millefiori Vase rubber stamp • Clear embossing ink • Deep Impression Clear embossing powder • Ivory acrylic paint • Clear button • 3/4" Lemon and Banana sheer ribbons • Metallic Gold marker • Gray chalk

Feminine Spring - MATERIALS: Black Millinery Mini Matts • Millefiori Bouquet rubber stamp • Clear embossing ink • Deep Impression Clear embossing powder • Ivory acrylic paint • 2 buttons • 12" piece of 1/4" Frost and Banana ribbons • Metallic Copper marker • Chalk (White, Green, Yellow)
TIPS: Attach buttons. Wrap and tie ribbons in bow. Apply heat tool to curl ribbon. Attach hat to head and pin back to finished piece.

Butterfly Soiree - MATERIALS: Black Rectangular Mini Matts • Grande Soiree rubber stamp • Gold pigment ink • Gold embossing powder • Ivory acrylic paint • Blue and Clear crystal beads • 8" pieces of 1/4" sheer ribbon (Frost, Aqua, Periwinkle) • Butterfly charm • Metallic Gold marker • Blue and White chalk
TIPS: Punch 3 holes in bottom. String beads on ribbons and tie through holes. Use heat tool to curl ribbons. Attach charm and pin back.

Crystal Blue Sensation - MATERIALS: White Mini Matts Rectangle • Pearl Beadwork rubber stamp • Silver pigment ink • Silver embossing powder • Pastel Blue acrylic paint • 22 gauge Silver wire • Pearl flower button • Beads (large and small Green pearl, White pearl, Blue glass, Silver) • Crystal drops • Translucent heart charm • Round-nose pliers • Silver metallic marker
TIPS: Punch 3 holes at bottom. Add dangles of Silver wire, beads, drops and charms. Remove shank from button with wire cutters and glue on front. Glue pin on back.

Antique Embossing™

Wall pockets with the look of embossed ceiling tiles are simply charming while faux ceramic tiles grace the lid of decorative as well as lovely and useful container!

Basic Instructions

MATERIALS: Rubber stamps • Clear embossing or pigment ink • Deep Impression™ Clear or metallic embossing powder • Acrylic paints • Heat tool • Paintbrush • Metallic markers • FabriTac™ • Terry cloth

TIPS: Apply Black paint over one side and let dry. Stamp on the painted surface and emboss. Apply second color of paint and let dry. Scrub paint from embossed areas with damp terry cloth.

Pocket Posies - MATERIALS: 5½" square metallic sheet • Beaded Bloom rubber stamp • Clear embossing ink • Deep Impression Clear embossing powder • Black and Cream acrylic paints • Wire (18 gauge galvanized, 22 gauge Purple or 24 gauge Silver) • Assorted buttons • Assorted pearl beads • ⅛" hole punch • Decorative scissors • Round-nose pliers • Metallic Gold marker

TIPS: Cut metal in fan shape. Trim edge with decorative scissors. Punch holes in scalloped areas for Cream posey. Apply Cream or Pink paint and let dry. Finish edges on Cream posey with marker. Roll into cone shape and glue seam. Let dry. Punch holes in sides and attach coiled galvanized wire and bead handle or Silver wire and button handle. Form loop of Purple wire, add buttons and beads and attach through punched hole in front of Cream posey and outline edge with marker.

Rose Heart - MATERIALS: 4" wood heart cut out • Rose Points and Leaf Trio rubber stamps • Clear embossing ink • Deep Impression Clear embossing powder • Black and Pastel Pink acrylic paints • 22 gauge Pink wire • Crystal heart • Pink button • Pink beads • Round-nose pliers • Craft drill and ⅛" bit • Metallic Copper marker

TIPS: Drill small holes at sides and attach coiled and beaded wire handle. Attach buttons and beads to front of heart. Color edge with marker.

Timeless Memoirs Tin - MATERIALS: Small tin • Timeless Memoirs rubber stamp • Clear embossing ink • Deep Impression Clear embossing powder • Acrylic paint (Brown, Pastel Blue, Cream) • Buttons • Old key • Postage stamp • Paintbrush • Metallic Gold marker

TIPS: Apply Brown paint and let dry. Stamp Timeless Memoirs and emboss. Blend Pastel Blue and Cream paints over tin and let dry. Highlight edges of tin with marker. Attach buttons, key and postage stamp.

Mini Pocket Posey

Mini Pocket Posey - MATERIALS: 3" square metallic sheet • Beaded Bloom rubber stamp • Clear embossing ink • Deep Impression Clear embossing powder • Black and Pastel Yellow acrylic paints • 22 gauge Copper wire • Buttons • Beads (Copper, Gold, Silver, Gold E) • 1/8" hole punch • Decorative scissors • Round-nose pliers • Metallic Copper marker

Scalloped Envelope

MATERIALS: Copper metallic sheet • Beaucoup de Papillons rubber stamp • Clear embossing ink • Deep Impression Clear embossing powder • Black and Pastel Peach acrylic paints • 22 gauge Copper wire • Buttons • Bead • 1/8" hole punch • Decorative scissors • Round-nose pliers • Metallic Copper marker
TIPS: Trace envelope on metal. Cut out. Trim top edge with decorative scissors. Punch holes in scalloped areas. Finish edges with marker. Fold bottom and sides in. Punch holes at sides and attach wire and bead handle. Attach buttons and coiled wire embellishment. Color edges with marker.

Tiled Art Tin

Tiled Art Tin - MATERIALS: Tin box with hinged lid • Ivory Shrinky Dinks • Rubber stamps (Tiled Quad Cube, Renaissance Frieze) • Top Boss Clear embossing ink • Brilliance inks (Pearlescent Crimson, Pearlescent Ice Blue, Pearlescent Ivy, Pearlescent Beige) • Deep Impression Clear embossing powder • Black and Ivory acrylic paints • Gray Liquid Applique • Earthtone Rub-Ons • Ivory double tassel • Braided trim • 2 filigree metal charms • Buttons • 3 postage stamps • Letter tiles • 4 large round beads • Heat tool • Terry cloth • Wood block • Talcum powder • Acrylic spray sealer
TIPS: Paint tin Black, let dry. Stamp Renaissance Frieze around sides of tin with Clear ink and emboss with Clear powder, rolling stamp around curves as necessary. Paint tin Ivory, let dry. Rub paint from embossed areas with damp terry cloth. Apply Rub-Ons with soft cloth. Cut Shrinky Dinks in 3" squares. Dust both sides with talcum powder. Pre-ink sides of tiled cube with Brilliance ink. Shrink squares with heat tool. While hot, immediately press inked stamp hard into plastic for Intaglio relief image. Repeat on all sides of cube using all 4 Brilliance colors, matching one color with one side of cube. Make enough to cover lid. Round corners by heating and cutting with scissors while warm. Adhere tiles to lid with FabriTac, let dry. Apply Liquid Applique as grout between tiles. Do not heat. Let dry 24 hours. Spray with sealer and let dry. Attach braided trim, tassel, charms, buttons and postage stamp. For feet, glue beads on bottom.

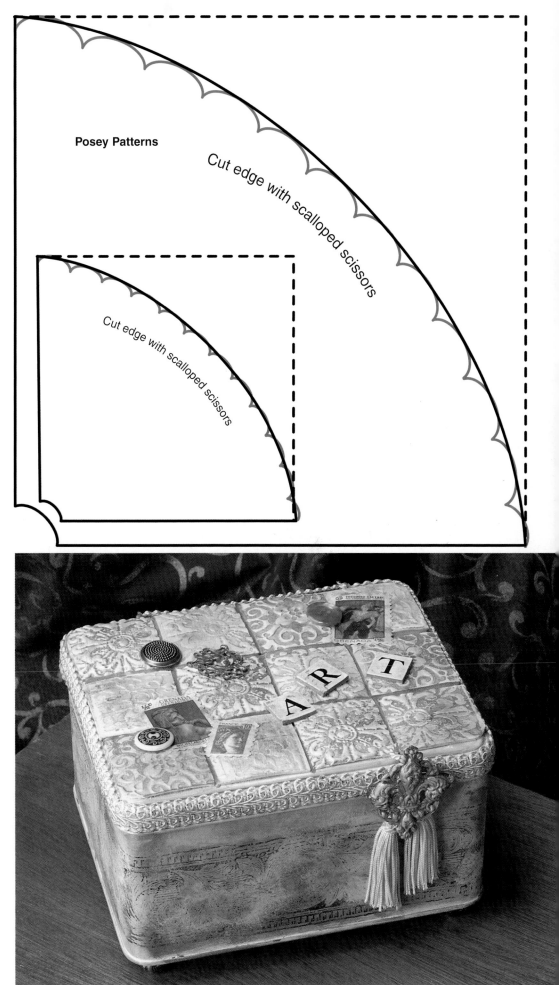

Posey Patterns

Envelope Pattern

Fold

Cut edge with scalloped scissors

Cut edge with scalloped scissors

Fold

Subtle colors and elegant designs make these projects suitable for Christmas or any season of the year!

Frame - MATERIALS: Wood frame • Black Mini Matts Oval • Foliage Quad Cube rubber stamp • Clear embossing ink • Deep Impression Clear and Gold embossing powder • Sage and Ivory acrylic paint • Gold number stickers • 2 Gold brads • 26 gauge Green wire • Red E beads • Hot Sheet
TIPS: Paint frame Ivory, stamp and emboss with Clear powder. Paint Sage, let dry and scrub off embossed areas with damp cloth. Punch holes in sides of oval. Place oval on Hot Sheet in pan heated to 300°F. Spoon on Clear embossing powder and let melt. Spoon on Gold powder, melt. Clean holes while still warm. Twist wires and attach beads. Attach oval to top of frame sandwiching wire ends and insert brads in holes. Apply number stickers.

Card - MATERIALS: Long Pewter card • Glossy Black cardstock • Rubber stamps (Pua Koa, Foliage Quad Cube, Tiled Quad Cube) • Top Boss Clear embossing ink • Deep Impression Clear embossing powder • Acrylic paint (Sage, Mauve, Hunter, Plum) • Gold Rub-Ons • Brads (star, 8 small round) • ¼" Pink and Burgundy sheer ribbon • Sticky Squares
TIPS: Stamp Pua Koa on card and emboss. Paint Sage, let dry. Cut tree, trunk and package shapes from cardstock. Stamp and emboss. Scrub paint off embossed areas with damp cloth. Attach tree with brads. Apply Rub-Ons. Attach package with Sticky Square. Tie bows and glue in place.

Tree Pattern

Candle - MATERIALS: Green pillar candle • Metallic sheet • Assorted texture rubber stamps • Deep Impression Clear embossing ink • Clear embossing powder • Acrylic paint (Black, Pink, Sage, Mauve, Cream) • 33 Silver brads • Metallic Rub-Ons
TIPS: Cut 2" metal squares paint Black, stamp and emboss. Paint with remaining colors, let dry and scrub paint off embossed areas with damp cloth. Apply Rub-Ons and attach squares with brads.

Boudoir Box - MATERIALS: Square tin • Rubber stamps (Thoughtful Heart Wood Set, Eau de Parfum, Tulip Trio) • Clear embossing ink • Deep Impression Clear embossing powder • Acrylic paint (Ivory, Pastel Yellow, Pastel Pink) • Assorted buttons • Assorted beads
TIPS: Paint tin Black, stamp and emboss. Paint, let dry and scrub off embossed areas with damp cloth. Attach buttons and beads.

Star Box - MATERIALS: Papier-mâché star box • Black Mini Matts Oval • Rubber stamps (Classic Plume, Floral Tile) • Clear embossing ink • Deep Impression Clear and Gold embossing powder • Sage and Black acrylic paint • Gold letter stickers • 2 Gold brads • Hot Sheet
TIPS: Paint box Black, stamp and emboss with Clear powder. Paint, let dry and scrub off embossed areas with damp cloth. Attach buttons and beads. Punch holes in sides of oval. Place oval on Hot Sheet in pan heated to 300°F. Spoon on Clear embossing powder and let melt. Spoon on Gold powder, melt. Clean holes while still warm. Attach to top of box and insert brads in holes. Apply letter stickers.

Crystal Chic Pin - MATERIALS: Black Mini Matts Rectangle • Geo Rose rubber stamp • Silver pigment ink • Silver embossing powder • Cream and Pastel Pink acrylic paint • Beads (6 Pink pearl, 5 Iridescent, 3 Crystal drop, 2 Crystal) • Pin back • Metallic Silver marker
TIPS: Attach beads through holes at top and bottom with Silver wire. Glue pin on back.

Bee Happy Garden Hanger - MATERIALS: Wood shape • Rubber stamps (Bee Happy, Floral Birdhouse, Ribbon Daisies, Lace Cluster, Pua Koa, Beaded Spray, Always Friends) • Clear embossing ink • Pine Ancient Page ink • Deep Impression Clear embossing powder • Broken terra cotta pottery • Acrylic paints (Black, Pastel Blue, Pastel Pink, Pastel Yellow, Ivory) • Colored pencils • 22 gauge Silver wire • Buttons • Beads • Metallic Copper marker • Craft drill and bit • Clear acrylic spray finish
TIPS: Spray pottery with finish, let dry. Paint wood plaque Black, let dry. Stamp wood and several pieces of pottery with Clear ink and emboss with Clear powder. Apply paints, let dry. Stamp Floral Birdhouse and Beaded Spray on pottery with Pine ink and color with pencils. Edge plaque with Copper marker. Drill 2 holes at top and 5 holes at bottom. Wrap pottery pieces with Silver wire, buttons and beads. Form loop at top of each piece. Attach Silver twisted wire hanger with button embellishment at top of plaque.

Package Shape

Antique Embossing™ with Wire, Buttons & Beads

Basic Instructions

MATERIALS: Black Mini Matts • Rubber stamps • Clear emboss-ing or pigment ink • Embossing powder • Acrylic paint • 22 gauge Silver wire • Paintbrush • Heat tool • 1/8" hole punch or drill bit • Needle-nose pliers • Chalk • Terry cloth

TIPS: Stamp designs on shapes with embossing ink and emboss. Apply paint, let dry. Rub paint from embossed areas with damp cloth. Apply chalk. Finish edges of pieces with marker. Punch holes. String beads and buttons on wire, attach pieces with twist-ed and coiled wire.

Beautiful Friend Hanging Treasure - MATERIALS: Large oval Black and Millinery Mini Matts • Rubber stamps (Beautiful Friend, Millefiori Vase, Millefiori Daisy) • Clear and Gold pigment inks • Gold embossing powder • Deep Impression Clear embossing powder • Ivory acrylic paint • Gold tinsel cord • Pearl buttons and beads • 3" of chain • Metallic Gold marker

TIPS: Stamp designs with Clear ink and emboss with Clear powder. Stamp and emboss designs on back of pieces with Gold ink and Gold powder. String beads and buttons on wire, attach pieces with twisted and coiled wire. Attach chain around waist. Tie cord hanging loop.

1. Wrap the wire around the selected piece.

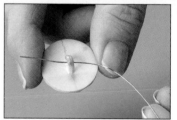

2. Add buttons or beads and secure by twisting wire.

3. Make spiral in end with round-nose pliers.

4. Secure piece by looping wire and twisting.

Asian Charm - MATERIALS: Black Mini Matts • Health Characters rubber stamp • Clear embossing ink • Deep Impression Clear embossing powder • Ivory acrylic paint • Buttons • Beads • Metallic Gold marker • Asian coin

TIPS: String beads and buttons on Silver wire, attach pieces with coiled and twisted wire. Glue buttons on shapes.

Acrylique Embossing™

Geo Botanica - MATERIALS: Black Geo Frame and White Triangle Mini Matts • Royal Orchid Script rubber stamp • Clear embossing ink • Vivid Yellow embossing powder • Carnelian PEARLustre • Acrylic paints (Purple, Mauve, Yellow, Orange, Lime) • 22 gauge Yellow wire • Metallic E beads • Wood bead • Paintbrush • Heat tool • 1/8" and 1/16" hole punches • Round-nose pliers • Pin back • Metallic Gold marker • FabriTac • Terry cloth

TIPS: Stamp triangle with Clear ink and emboss with PEARLustre. Paint design, let dry. Scrub paint from embossed areas with damp terry cloth. Stamp frame with Clear ink and emboss with Vivid Yellow powder. Finish edges with Gold marker. Punch holes and attach pieces with coils of wire threaded with beads. Adhere pin back.

Traditional, mod art or Oriental... find a theme to suit every taste.

1. Apply the Yellow background paint.

2. Stamp design with Clear ink and emboss with PEARLustre powders.

3. Using the lightest color first, blend wet-on-wet splotches of color and let dry.

4. Gently scrub paint from embossed areas.

5. Add postage stamps, wire and other embellishments.

6. Attach easel pieces.

Bring art to your office with a unique note board and a handy file card box!

Orchid Booklace
MATERIALS: 2 White Geo Frame Mini Matts • Paper • Purebeck Gold Orchid rubber stamp • Clear embossing ink • Amethyst PEARLustre embossing powder • 24 gauge Purple wire • E beads • 34" of satin cord • Paintbrush • Heat tool • 1/16" hole punch • Photo • Watercolor pencils • Metallic Gold marker • Needle-nose pliers

TIPS: Stamp design and emboss with PEARLustre. Use wet paintbrush and pencils to color design. Finish edges with marker. Cut pages to fit frame. Decorate pages as desired. Punch holes along edges of pages and frame. Thread beads on wire and coil wire through holes. Attach photo to back of frame. Fold cord in half and insert through hole. Add beads and tie overhand knot at ends.

Palette de Artiste
MATERIALS: White Mini Matts • Rubber stamps (Artistic Impressions Brushes wood stamp set, Millefiori Cluster, Millefiori Heart) • Clear embossing ink • Vivid Yellow embossing powder • Acrylic paints (Red, Blue, White, Yellow) • Beads (large flower, large Orange bead, assorted E) • 24 gauge Blue wire • Pin back • Paintbrush • Heat tool • 1/16" hole punch • Round-nose pliers • Metallic Gold marker • FabriTac

TIPS: Stamp designs with Clear ink and emboss with Vivid Yellow powder over all pieces as desired. Mix paints and apply to designs with brush. Let dry. Punch holes. Finish edges with marker. Thread beads on wire and embellish with coiled and twisted wire. Adhere pin back.

Botanica Treasure Box
MATERIALS: Unfinished wood box • Rubber stamps (Primitive Fringe, Floral Textile, Floral Diamond, Orchid Elements, Wyatt Orchid) • Clear embossing ink • PEARLustre (Adventurine, Carnelian, Amethyst, Hessonite) • Acrylic paints (Lavender, Yellow, Teal, Orange) • Metallic Rub-Ons • Postage stamps • 3 buttons • Pearl-topped straight pin • Beads (5 large Terra Cotta, Gold) • Gold charm • Flat glass marble • Paintbrush • Heat tool • FabriTac • Terry cloth

TIPS: Paint the inside of box Lavender and outside Yellow, let dry. Stamp and emboss with various powders. Apply splotches of paint over box, let dry. Scrub away paint from embossed areas with damp cloth. Apply Rub-Ons for highlights. Adhere postage stamps, buttons and charm to lid. Layer flat button, large bead and Gold bead with adhesive and insert straight pin. Glue 4 beads to bottom for feet, let dry.

Embossed Box
MATERIALS: Wood box with hinge • Copper metallic sheet • Rubber stamps (Acorn Leaves, Laurel Leaf Border, Floral Tile) • Clear embossing ink • Jet Black StazOn ink • Deep Impression Clear embossing powder • Acrylic paints (Ivory, Russet) • Copper Metallic Rub-Ons • Stylus • Paintbrush • Heat tool • Acrylic spray sealer • Removable tape • FabriTac • Terry cloth

TIPS: Paint box Ivory, let dry. Stamp Floral Tile with Clear ink and emboss. Stamp and emboss Laurel Leaf on corners. Place strips of tape around lid to mask, stamp and emboss Acorn Leaves on center of lid. Remove tape, stamp and emboss Laurel Leaf border masking corners for miter effect. Paint box Russet, let dry and scrub paint from embossed areas. Apply Rub-Ons highlights. Stamp Acorn leaves on Silver side of metallic sheet with Black ink and trace with stylus to deboss design. Brush the Copper side with Black ink and apply Rub-Ons to highlight embossed areas. Cut to fit front of box, glue in place and spray box with sealer.

Note board
MATERIALS: Framed corkboard • Wood handle box • Rubber stamps (Wyatt Orchid, Floral Diamond, Purebeck Gold Orchid, Orchid Expressions, Primitive Fringe, Floral Textile, Mendhi Moth, Mini Moth) • Top Boss Clear embossing ink • Ink (Sandalwood, Mandarin and Lavender Ancient Page, Black Crafters, Black StazOn) • Deep Impression Clear embossing powder • Acrylic paint (Ivory, Periwinkle, Crimson, Poppy, Orange, Yellow, Lime) • Dimensional Magic • Earthtones Rub-Ons • White Shrinky Dinks • Pencils and notepaper • Thumb tacks • Buttons • Postage stamps • Brass charm • 26 gauge wire (Blue, Purple, Orange) • Ivory double tassel • Paintbrush • Heat tool • 1/8" hole punch • Talcum powder • Acrylic spray sealer • Fabrico markers • Super glue • FabriTac • Terry cloth

TIPS:

Corkboard. Stamp images on cork with Black Crafters ink masking if necessary. Set with heat tool. Mask off cork and paint frame Ivory, let dry. Stamp with Clear ink and emboss Floral Texture on front and Floral Diamond on sides with Clear powder. Brush with various colors of paint, let dry and scrub off embossed areas with damp terry cloth. Apply Rub-Ons. Spray with sealer, let dry. Decorate box using the same technique. Glue on buttons, charm and stamps. Roll pencils across inked stamp and embossing powder and paint to match box. Tie tassel around one pencil. Stamp notepaper with Floral Textile and Ancient Page inks. Glue box on edge of frame and insert note paper and pencils.

Tacks. Stamp Mendhi Moth, Primitive Fringe and Purebeck Gold Orchid on Shrinky Dinks with Black StazOn ink. Set ink slightly with heat tool. Color with markers and cut out. Sprinkle talcum powder on both sides, punch holes in fringe pieces and moth. Shrink pieces shaping over pencil while warm. Add wire fringe and antennae in holes. Brush with Dimensional Magic and let dry. Super Glue on thumb tacks.

Spotlight your favorite picture in a frame that matches the photo theme!

Exotic Botanica Frame

Exotic Botanica Frame - MATERIALS: White craft frame • White Mini Matts • Rubber stamps (Purebeck Gold Orchid, Mini Moth) • Clear embossing ink • Vivid Yellow embossing powder • Acrylic paints (Aqua, Teal, Orange, Red, Purple, Magenta, Dark Green) • 24 gauge Copper wire • Assorted beads • Button • Variegated raffia • Paintbrush • 1/8" hole punch • Sticky Squares • Round-nose pliers

TIPS: Paint frame Aqua, let dry. Apply other colors in splotches and stripes, let dry. Apply splotches of paints to Mini Matts, let dry. Stamp designs with Clear ink and emboss with Yellow powder. Punch holes in matts. Attach raffia tassel, small matt pieces and button to square with coiled wire threaded with beads. Tie several strands of raffia to top of frame, add beads.

Raffia Ties

1. Fold six to eight 8" raffia strands in half.

2. Wrap with wire and attach to frame.

Wild Botanica Frame

Wild Botanica Frame - MATERIALS: Black craft frame • Black Mini Matts Rectangle • Rubber stamps (Orchid Elements, Royal Orchid Script, Floral Textile) • Clear embossing ink • Embossing powders (Amethyst, Carnelian, Azurite PEARLustre) • Acrylic paints (Yellow, Mustard, Pink, Red, White, Teal, Green, Purple) • Button • 22 gauge Red wire • Assorted beads • Postage stamp • 1/8" hole punch • Round-nose pliers • Paintbrush • Glue • Terry cloth

TIPS: Paint frame Yellow. Stamp designs with Clear ink and emboss with various powders. Apply paint splotches all over frame and Mini Matt, let dry. Scrub paint from embossed areas using damp cloth. Adhere postage stamp to frame. Punch holes in matt and attach to frame with coiled wire threaded with beads.

Under the Sea Frame

Under the Sea Frame - MATERIALS: Black craft frame • Frost Shrinky Dinks • Rubber stamps (Seashell Points, Barry Reef, Cora Reef) • Clear embossing ink • Neptune Ancient Page ink • Sapphire PEARLustre • Acrylic paints (Medium Blue, Pink, White, Purple, Lime, Dark Green) • Paintbrush • Postage stamps • Clear rubber bubble dots • 22 gauge Burgundy wire • Buttons • Assorted beads • Heat tool • 1/4" hole punch • Round-nose pliers • Sponge • Talcum powder • Glue • Terry cloth

TIPS: Stamp Barry Reef and Cora Reef on frame with Clear embossing ink and emboss with Sapphire powder. Apply splotches of paint and add details around designs, let dry. Gently scrub paint from embossed areas with damp cloth. Adhere postage stamps and bubble dots. Cut shell from Shrinky Dinks. Rub talcum powder over both sides and wipe off with paper towel. Sponge edges with ink to highlight shell shape. Stamp Seashell Points with Neptune ink. Punch holes in base. Shrink with heat tool. Attach shell, buttons and beads to top of frame with twists of wire.

Shell Pattern

A carnival of shapes and colors is yours when you make this unusual box filled with hanging ornaments!

Carnival Box

MATERIALS: Wood divided cigar box • Black Millinery Mini Matts • Scrap paper • White glossy cardstock • Rubber stamps (Catapult, Cateroboics, Plume Points, Wavy Keys, Dotted Border, Prancing Zebra, Words of Friendship, Geo Square Orb, Wavy Music, Tiger Pair, Peacock Fan, Dotted Frame) • Clear embossing ink • Inks (Coal and Sandalwood Ancient Page, Black ColorBox) • Deep Impression Black embossing powder • Acrylic paints (Black, Blue, Purple, Teal) • Gold Rub-Ons • Ultra Fine glitter (Blue, Lavender) • Mint Magic Mesh • Postage stamps • Assorted wire • Assorted beads • Assorted fibers • Feathers • Assorted rhinestones • Diamond Dots • 4 small cup hooks • Sponge • Spray sealer • FabriTac • Mrs. Glue • Terry cloth

TIPS:

Box. Paint outside of box Black, let dry. Stamp and emboss images. Brush various paints on box, let dry and wipe off embossed areas with damp cloth. Paint inside of box in desired colors, let dry. Stamp images on White paper with Coal ink. Tear out and glue inside box with Mrs. Glue. Brush glue in other areas and sprinkle with glitters. Add postage stamps, rhinestones and Magic Mesh. Spray with sealer.

Ornaments. Stamp and emboss Mini Matts, brush with paint and wipe off embossed areas with damp cloth. Apply Rub-Ons to edges. Thread beads on wire, twist and coil and place on head for hair. Make wire and bead dangles and add to bottom of head. Add feathers, fibers, beads and wire to torso. Stamp and emboss cats and zebra on cardstock. Cut out and add glitter and Diamond Dots. Attach cats to wire hanger and zebra to a wire pole. Screw cup hooks in top of compartments and hang ornaments. Glue beads on bottom of box for feet. Tie fibers on latch.

Basic Instructions

MATERIALS: Frosted Shrinky Dinks® • Rubber stamps • Brilliance ink • Chalk • Heat tool • 1/4" hole punch • Wire cutters • Round-nose pliers • Wood block • Talcum powder • Paper towels

1. Cut freeform shape from 1/4 sheet of shrink plastic. Rub talcum over both sides and wipe off with paper towel. Punch hole and stamp design on smooth side.

2. Color on rough side of plastic with chalk.

3. Shrink with heat tool, flatten with wood block.

4. Embellish plastic with wire and beads.

Posey Jar - MATERIALS: Glass jar • Rubber stamps (Pansy Patch, Nymph Butterfly) • Victorian Violet Brilliance ink • Wire (18 gauge galvanized, 22 gauge Purple) • Assorted beads
TIPS: Stamp the designs with Violet ink. Color with chalk. Thread beads on galvanized wire and wrap and coil wire to create a hanger. Wrap Purple wire around the large shrink piece and attach to the jar. Thread the beads on Purple wire and attach smaller pieces with twisted wire.

Pendant - MATERIALS: Rubber stamps (Grow With Love, Suzanne Bouquet) • Victorian Violet Brilliance ink • 22 gauge Gold wire • Assorted beads • Leaf and flower beads • 30" pieces (1/8" Teal and Fuchsia ribbon, fine Gold cord) • FabriTac
TIPS: Stamp saying and design on smooth side. Heat set ink slightly. Color with chalk. Shrink. Attach cord and ribbon with jump ring. Coil wire threaded with beads and add to bottom. Thread beads on cord and ribbon, knot ends to secure. Tie ends together. Glue flower and leaf beads on front.

Frosted Shrink Plastic

Seashell Points Pin - MATERIALS: White Shrinky Dinks • Rubber stamps (Seashell Points, Sunrise/Sunset) • Neptune Ancient Page ink • Large Silver jump rings • Silver Itty Bitty Beads • Tiny shells • Bits of sea glass • Sponge • Pin back • FabriTac

TIPS: Sprinkle talcum powder over White shrink plastic and wipe off excess. Stamp Sunrise/Sunset and cut out. Punch holes. Cut freeform shape from Frost shrink plastic. Rub talcum powder over both sides and wipe off. Stamp designs and sponge edges with ink. Punch holes. Shrink. Attach pieces with jump rings. Glue beads, shells, glass and pin back in place, let dry.

> **Hint.** Dusting with talcum powder eliminates sanding to add tooth. Sprinkle on and wipe away with a paper towel, soft cloth or a clean brush. Too much powder or not dusting will interfere with the inks. Powder keeps shrink plastic from sticking to itself when heated. A hole in the plastic and a wire hook can help hold the piece when heating.

Star Bookmark - MATERIALS: Shrink Silhouette Star • Rubber stamps (Large Wire Snowflake, Snowflake Flurry) • Sky Blue Brilliance ink • Assorted beads • 20 gauge Silver wire • ⅝" White satin ribbon • Silver tassel • Silver jump ring • Metallic Silver marker

TIPS: Stamp Large Wire Snowflake on star, shrink. Color edges with marker. Stamp ribbon with Snowflake Flurry. Thread beads on coiled wire, attach to top and bottom of star. Tie one end of ribbon to jump ring and tassel to other end, attach to star.

Heart Card - MATERIALS: Dark Blue cardstock (4¼" x 5½" card, 2¼" square) • Shrink Silhouette Heart • Rubber stamps (Snow Swirl, Small Wire Snowflake) • Brilliance ink (Moonlight White, Mediterranean Blue) • Ultra Fine Silver glitter • Double sided adhesive

TIPS: Stamp Snow Swirl on card with Moonlight White. Cut 2 thin strips of adhesive, place as shown. Sprinkle with glitter. Stamp Wire Snowflake on heart and stipple edges with Mediterranean Blue, shrink. Apply glitter to edge of 2½" square with adhesive. Attach square and heart.

Tile Card - MATERIALS: Cardstock (4¼" x 5½" Tan card, 3¼" x 4½" torn Green) • Shrinky Dinks (Ivory, Brown) • Rubber stamps (Floral Tile, Laurel Leaf Border, Renaissance Frieze, Tiled Quad Cube, Faux Finish Quad Cube) • Pearlescent Brilliance ink (Beige, Crimson, Ivy) • Dimensional Magic • 24 gauge Copper wire • Assorted beads • Charm • Pin back • ⅛" hole punch

TIPS: Stamp Tan cardstock with Faux Finish Cube in Crimson. Stamp Beige Renaissance Frieze on Brown Shrinky Dinks. Stamp Crimson Floral Tile on Ivory. Stamp Ivy Laurel Leaf Border around tile. Heat set inks. Talcum and punch hole, shrink pieces. Brush Dimensional Magic on pieces. Layer and attach with Dimensional Magic. Place charm on tile and let dry. Thread beads on coil and attach. Attach pin back. Layer cardstock pieces and attach pin.

Heart Pin - MATERIALS: White Shrinky Dinks • Rubber stamps (Classic Plume, Renaissance Frieze, Tiled Quad Cube,) • Crimson and Pearlescent Beige Brilliance ink • Copper embossing powder • Charm • 2 buttons •

Assorted beads • Postage stamp • 24 gauge Gold wire • Deckle scissors • FabriTac

TIPS: Cut freeform shape with deckle scissors and heart. Stamp freeform piece with images, shrink. Shrink heart. Impress Tiled quad cube side pre-inked with Pearlescent Beige ink while warm. Attach piece and embellishments. Thread beads on wire, coil and attach.

Bookmark - MATERIALS: White Shrink Silhouette Oval • Harvest Leaf rubber stamp • Crafters ink (Ivy, Crimson) • Copper embossing powder • Assorted beads • 24 gauge Copper wire • 1" wire edge Copper ribbon • Ivory tassel • Metallic Copper marker

TIPS: Sprinkle Copper embossing powder on edges of oval. Shrink. Apply inks to stamp, stamp oval while still warm. Stipple Ivy ink on edges, heat set. Highlight edges with marker. String beads on wire, coil and attach to top and bottom of oval. Tie tassel and thread bead on one end of ribbon. Tie oval on other end.

Shrink Plastic

Make a fashion statement with lovely pins and bookmarks embellished with stamped images, ribbon and beads!

MATERIALS: Shrinky Dinks • Rubber stamps • Brilliance ink • Heat tool • Hole punch • Wire cutters • Round-nose pliers • Wood block • Talcum powder • Paper towels

1. Cut freeform shape from ¼ sheet of shrink plastic and dust with talcum powder.

2. Stamp design, punch hole.

3. Heat set briefly. Color with chalk.

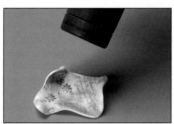

4. Shrink with heat tool.

5. Embellish with postage stamps, beads and wire.

Heart Bookmark - MATERIALS: White Shrink Silhouette Heart • Rubber stamps (Christmas Sentiments, Faceted Ornament, Cathy's Bow) • Red and Green Brilliance ink • Assorted Red and Green beads • 24 gauge Gold wire • ¼" hole punch • 1½" Red plaid ribbon • White tassel • Metallic Gold marker
TIPS: Dust with talcum powder, stamp designs on heart, shrink. Highlight edge with marker. Thread beads on wire and coil. Attach to top and bottom of heart. Coil end of top wire around one end of ribbon and tie tassel on other end.

Angel Card - MATERIALS: Cardstock (3" x 5½" Metallic Gold, 2¼" x 4" torn Green, 2" x 4" torn Red) • Black and White Shrinky Dinks • Angelica rubber stamp • Black Brilliance ink • 24 gauge Red wire • Gold and Crystal beads • ¼" hole punch • Gold Borders Class A'Peels • Ultra Fine Crystal glitter • Pin back • Fabrico markers • FabriTac • Mrs. Glue
TIPS: Dust talcum powder on White plastic, stamp angel, cut out and color with markers. Cut out Black plastic rectangle. Shrink. Apply glue to wings and sprinkle with glitter. Add border to Black piece and attach angel. Thread beads on coiled wire and attach. Layer cardstock and attach pin.

Always & Forever Memento Pin - MATERIALS: Brown Shrinky Dinks • Rubber stamps (Always and Forever, Stitched Heart) • Moonlight White Brilliance ink • Red Hearts Class A'Peels • Beaded fringe • Tiny photo • Pin back • Metallic Silver marker • FabriTac
TIPS: Cut freeform shape, rub with talcum powder and stamp designs. Shrink. Finish edges with marker. Adhere photo and fringe. Embellish with heart stickers. Adhere pin back.

Royal Chintz Pins - MATERIALS:
White Shrinky Dinks • Rubber stamps (Suzanne Bouquet, Friend Bouquet, Ribbon Daisies) • Mediterranean Blue Brilliance ink • 24 gauge Silver wire • Assorted beads • Assorted buttons • Blue Magic Mesh • Postage stamps • Pin back • Metallic Silver marker • ¼" hole punch • FabriTac

TIPS: Cut out the freeform shape, punch holes and dust with talcum powder. Stamp designs with Blue ink. Heat set slightly. Shade with chalk and shrink. Finish edges with marker. Embellish with postage stamps, Magic Mesh, buttons, wire and beads.

Fringed Tigers Pin - MATERIALS:
Ivory Shrinky Dinks • Rubber stamps (Tiger Pair, Moroccan Screen) • Black and Coffee Bean Brilliance inks • Postage stamps • 24 gauge Blue wire • Beads (bugle, E) • Pin back • ⅛" hole punch • Round-nose pliers • Metallic Gold marker • FabriTac

TIPS: Rub talcum powder over both sides and wipe off excess. Cut shape, stamp designs and punch holes. Shrink with heat tool. Embellish with coiled wire and beads. Adhere postage stamp and pin back.

Antique Ivory Christmas Pin - MATERIALS:
Ivory Shrinky Dinks • Gloria rubber stamp • Coffee Bean Brilliance ink • 22 gauge Gold wire • Beads • Postage stamp • ¼" hole punch • Sponge • Pin back • Metallic Copper marker • FabriTac

TIPS: Cut plastic, punch hole and dust with talcum powder. Sponge edges and stamp designs with ink. Shrink. Finish edge with marker. Embellish with twisted wire threaded with beads. Adhere postage stamps and pin back.

Ivory Collage Pin - MATERIALS:
Ivory Shrinky Dinks • Rubber stamps (Always and Forever, Eau de Parfum) • Coffee Bean Brilliance ink • Pin back • Tiny photo • Postage stamps • Red hearts Class A'Peels • Pin back • Sponge • FabriTac

TIPS: Cut heart and dust with talcum powder. Sponge edges and stamp the designs with ink and heat set. Shrink. Adhere the photo, postage stamps, stickers and pin back.

Heart Bookmark - MATERIALS:
White Shrink Silhouette Heart • Floral rubber stamp • Victorian Violet Brilliance ink • Assorted beads • Butterfly button • 26 gauge Green wire • ¼" square punch • 1½" Green sheer ribbon • Gold tassel

TIPS: Dust with talcum powder, punch holes as shown, stamp designs on heart, shrink. Thread beads on wire, coil. Attach to top and bottom of heart. Coil end of top wire around one end of ribbon. Tie tassel and thread beads and button on other end.

Butterfly Pin - MATERIALS:
White Shrinky Dinks • Pansy Patch rubber stamp • Victorian Violet Brilliance ink • 24 gauge Silver wire • Assorted beads • Postage stamp • Pin back • Metallic Silver marker • ¼" hole punch • Chalk • FabriTac

TIPS: Cut freeform shape, punch holes and dust with talcum powder. Stamp designs. Heat set slightly. Shade with chalk and shrink. Finish edges with marker. Add postage stamp. Thread beads on wire, coil and attach to bottom. Glue pin back in place.

DEEP DISH EMBEDDING™

This technique achieves the look of artifacts enclosed in glass. Add the finishing touches with wire and beads!

with Shrink Plastic

Basic Instructions

MATERIALS: Shrinky Dinks • Rubber stamps • Permanent ink • Deep Impression Clear embossing powder • Metallic sheet • Heat tool • Hot Sheet • Craft pan • ¼" hole punch • Round-nose pliers • Chalk • Talcum powder

1. Cut shrink plastic shape, punch hole and dust with talcum powder. Stamp image with permanent ink.

2. Briefly heat set. Color with chalk. Shrink with heat tool.

3. Mold metallic sheet around shrunken shape.

4. Place in pan heated to 300°F and spoon in Deep Impression Clear embossing powder. Melt.

5. Inset embellishments and layer with more powder.

6. Remove from pan, let cool. Remove metallic sheet, place piece on a Hot Sheet and apply heat tool along sides to slump.

7. Clean punched holes and add embellishments.

Note: Recommended permanent inks include Brilliance, Ancient Page, Crafter's Ink and Memories. Brilliance ink will not bleed or change colors when subjected to heat. Ancient Page or Memories ink darken with heat and the colors will sometimes float in the melted embossing powder for an interesting effect. When slumping, it is important to hold heat tool horizontal to the piece and parallel to the work surface. Do not heat from the top or image will melt unevenly.

Black Plume Pin - MATERIALS: Black Shrinky Dinks • Classic Plume Rubber stamp • Gold Brilliance ink • Foil (Pearl Splash, Rainbow Blend) • 24 gauge Gold wire • Assorted beads
TIPS: Cut, stamp, shrink plastic and make Deep Dish shape. Crumple foils to create pattern. Spot heat plastic, protect fingers with towel and press foil on hot spot and lift. Repeat as desired. Finish Deep Dish shape. Add wire and bead dangle.

Dichroic Glass Pendant - MATERIALS: Black Shrinky Dinks • Rainbow Blend Foil • 24 gauge Blue wire • 36" of Black and 72" of Blue Iridescent cord • Blue bead
TIPS: Cut, shrink plastic and make Deep Dish shape. Crumple foil to create pattern. Spot heat plastic, protect fingers with towel and press foil on hot spot and lift. Repeat as desired. Finish Deep Dish shape. Embellish with wire and bead using wire to form bail. Thread cords through bail and tie knots.

Ocean Pin - MATERIALS: Black Shrinky Dinks • Foil scraps • Gold Itty Bitty Beads • Shells • Charm • Pin back • Metallic Gold marker • FabriTac
TIPS: Cut, shrink plastic and make Deep Dish shape. Insert charm shells, foil scraps and beads in melted powder. Finish Deep Dish shape. Finish edges with Gold marker. Adhere pin back.

Heart Pin - MATERIALS: Black Shrinky Dinks • Rubber stamps (Rose Lace Collage, Hands and Heart) • Moonlight White Brilliance ink • Ribbons and Bows Class A' Peel border • Charm • 22 gauge Gold wire • Heart rhinestone • Gold and Pearl beads • Pin back • FabriTac
TIPS: Cut, stamp and shrink plastic. Insert border and charm in melted powder. Finish Deep Dish shape. Add beads and wire dangle. Adhere heart and pin back.

Floral Tile Pendant - MATERIALS: Black Shrinky Dinks • Floral Tile rubber stamp • Copper Brilliance ink • Rainbow Blend Foil • 22 gauge Copper wire • 36" of Black cord • 2 Purple beads
TIPS: Cut, stamp, shrink plastic and make Deep Dish shape. Crumple foil to create pattern. Spot heat plastic, protect fingers with towel and press foil on hot spot and lift. Repeat as desired. Finish deep dish shape. Embellish with wire and beads.

Prancing Zebra - MATERIALS: Bright White Shrinky Dinks • Rubber stamps (Prancing Zebra, Palm Fronds, Kenya Cluster) • Brilliance inks (Pearlescent Jade, Coral, Yellow) • Black Magic Mesh • Beads (assorted seed, Yellow bugle, Pink, Blue E) • Button • 26 gauge Blue wire • Pin back • FabriTac

Deep Dish Africa - MATERIALS: White Shrinky Dinks • Rubber stamps (Prancing Zebra, Kenya Montage, Palm Fronds) • Brilliance inks (Coffee Bean, Gamma Green) • 22 gauge Gold wire • Gold Itty Bitty Beads • Assorted beads • Flat glass marble • Leaf charm • Feathers • Pin back • Chalk • FabriTac
TIPS: Cut, stamp, color, shrink plastic and make Deep Dish shape. Insert marble, charm and Gold beads. Finish Deep Dish shape. Add wire and beads. Glue feathers and pin on back.

Zebra - MATERIALS: White Shrinky Dinks • Rubber stamps (Prancing Zebra, Palm Fronds, Kenya Cluster) • Ancient Page inks (Neptune, Cardinal, Lime, Sienna) • Black Magic Mesh • Assorted seed and bugle beads • 22 gauge Copper wire • Pin back • FabriTac

Orchid Pendant - MATERIALS: Ruff n' Ready Shrinky Dinks • Wyatt Orchid rubber stamp • Lavender Ancient Page ink • Postage stamp • Assorted beads (flower, seed, pony) • Beaded trim • 1/16" Turquoise ribbon • FabriTac
TIPS: Cut, punch 2 holes at top, stamp and shrink plastic. Insert postage stamp and seed and flower beads. Finish deep dish shape. Add pony beads and ribbon to hole. Glue beaded trim on bottom.

Blue Plume - MATERIALS: Ruff n' Ready Shrinky Dinks • Classic Plume rubber stamp • Turquoise Ancient Page ink • Foil (Pearl Splash, Rainbow Blend) • Gold bail • Turquoise ribbon • FabriTac
TIPS: Cut and shrink plastic. Crumple foils to create pattern. Spot heat plastic, protect fingers with towel, press foil on hot spot and lift. Repeat as desired. Finish deep dish shape. Glue bail on top, thread wire through bail and tie.

Friendship Pendant - MATERIALS: Frost Shrinky Dinks • Post Collage rubber stamp • Black Brilliance ink • Postage stamp • Wire (22 gauge Green, 26 gauge Turquoise) • Pony beads • Flower button • Lavender Ultra Fine glitter • 30" of White satin cord • Chalk
TIPS: Cut, punch 2 holes, stamp, color and shrink plastic. Insert postage stamp and button and sprinkle with glitter. Finish Deep Dish shape. Add wire hanger, satin cord and beads.

Under the Sea - MATERIALS: Ruff n' Ready Shrinky Dinks • Seashell Points rubber stamp • Turquoise Ancient Page ink • Charm • Sea shells • Assorted beads • Silver Itty Bitty Beads • Postage stamp • 30" of Gold cord • 2 Gold jump rings
TIPS: Cut, punch holes, shrink plastic and make deep dish shape. Insert postage stamp, shells, beads and Silver beads. Finish Deep Dish shape. Attach charm with jump ring. Add bead and cord.

more Deep Dish ideas on the following pages!

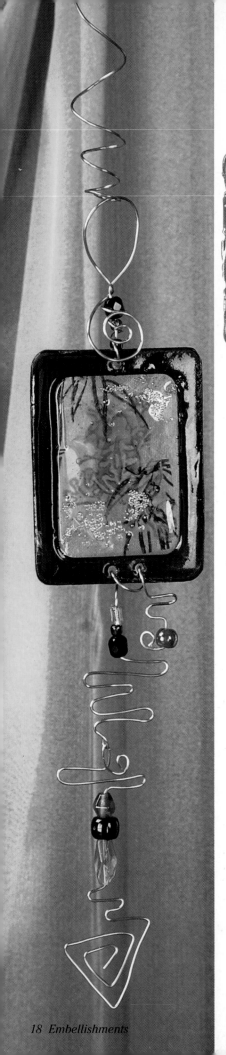

Suspend treasures in 'framed glass' for hangers that catch the eye as well as the sun!

DEEP DISH™ EMBEDDING with Shrink Plastic

Basic Instructions

MATERIALS: Mini Matts • Thermo acetate • Deep Impression Clear embossing powder • Craft pan • Hot Sheet • Round-nose pliers • 1/8" hole punch

1. Punch holes in frame. Place on Hot Sheet in pan, cover with Deep Impression powder and melt at 300°F.

2. Stamp design on acetate insert and color.

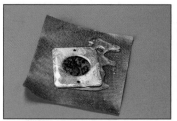

3. Insert acetate piece in melted powder and add more powder, melt. Sprinkle with glitter, remove from pan and let cool.

4. Clean holes while warm. Add wire and bead hanger and embellishments.

Jungle Froglet - MATERIALS: Black Geo Mini Matts Frame • Rubber stamps (Froglet, Bamboo) • Pine and Coal Ancient Page inks • Silver Itty Bitty Beads • 22 gauge Copper wire • Assorted beads
TIPS: Punch holes in frame, place in pan, sprinkle with powder and melt. Stamp acetate and insert in frame. Add Silver beads. Sprinkle with more powder, melt. Make hanger and dangles with wire and beads.

Swimming Froglet - MATERIALS: Black Geo Mini Matts Frame • Rubber stamps (Froglet, Frond Border) • Black and Moonlight Brilliance inks • Sky Blue and Jade Pearlescent Brilliance re-inkers • Multi Ultra Fine Crystal glitter • 24 gauge Green wire • Silver Itty Bitty Beads • Assorted beads • Leaf charm • Dimensional Magic • Tissue paper
TIPS: Stamp Froglet on acetate, heat set. Turn over and swirl dots of Dimensional Magic, re-inkers and glitter with fingertip. Crumple tissue and place over wet area, pressing to soak in. Let dry. Stamp Frond Border on frame with Moonlight. Punch holes. Place acetate piece in frame, sprinkle with powder and melt. Sprinkle with Silver beads and more powder, melt. Make hanger and dangle with wire, charm and beads.

Captured Artifact - MATERIALS: Black Mini Matts Geo Frame • PEARLustre powders (Carnelian, Amethyst, Adventurine) • Deep Impression Clear embossing powder • Black double tassel • Blue bead • Old coin • Pin back • FabriTac
TIPS: Punch holes, place in pan, sprinkle with powder, melt. Insert coin, add more powder, melt. Fold tassel in half and insert loop through bead and holes in matt. Tie under bead. Adhere pin back.

Shimmering Dragonflies - MATERIALS: Rubber stamps (Dotted Dragonfly, Small Dot Dragonfly, Dotted Border) • Brilliance re-inkers (Black, Moonlight, Sky Blue, Jade Pearlescent Brilliance) • Black Brilliance Ink • Multi Ultra Fine Crystal glitter • Silver metallic scrap • 22 gauge Silver wire • E beads • Silver Itty Bitty Beads • Dimensional Magic • Tissue paper
TIPS: Stamp designs on acetate, heat set. Turn over, swirl dots of Dimensional Magic, re-inkers and glitter with fingertip. Crumple tissue, place over wet area pressing to soak in. Let dry. Stamp Dotted Border on frame with Moonlight. Place acetate piece under frame in pan, sprinkle with powder, melt. Sprinkle with Silver beads and more powder, melt. Wrap with wire and beads.

Under the Sea Suncatcher

MATERIALS: White Mini Matts Geo Frames • Rubber stamps (Cora Reef, Limpet Points, Seashell Points, Koa Branch) • Brilliance inks (Mediterranean Blue, Jade, Sky Blue, Yellow Pearlescent) • 22 gauge Silver wire • Silver Itty Bitty Beads • Assorted beads (Crystal, flower, pony) • IdentiPens

TIPS: Punch holes and color frames with various inks. Stamp designs with Mediterranean Blue. Place in pan, sprinkle with powder and melt. Stamp Cora Reef and Limpet Points on acetate, heat set. Color backs with pens and insert in melted powder. Add more powder, melt. Sprinkle with Silver beads. Make hanger, dangle and connector with wire and beads.

Star Suncatcher

MATERIALS: White Geo Frame Mini Matts • Texture rubber stamps • Brilliance inks (Mediterranean Blue, Sky Blue) • 22 gauge Silver wire • Assorted beads • Snowflakes Class A'Peels • Glitter (Multi Ultra Fine, Blue Crystal Stars)

TIPS: Punch hole in large frame. Color frames with inks. Place in pan, small frame in large frame. Sprinkle with powder and melt. Add stickers and Star glitter. Add more powder and melt. Cut acetate star, color with inks place in pan, sprinkle with powder and melt. Add Multi glitter and more powder, melt. Remove and stamp with Texture while still hot. Make hanger, dangle and connector with wire and beads.

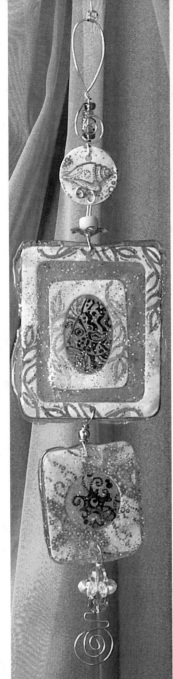

African Mask Suncatcher

MATERIALS: White Mini Matt Geo Frames • Rubber stamps (African Mask, Lioness Collage, Congo Border) • Brilliance inks (Black, Copper, Coffee Bean, Lightening Black) • 22 gauge Copper wire • Assorted beads • Feathers • Fibers • Italian paper clip • Gold Itty Bitty Beads • Glue

TIPS: Sprinkle with talcum powder, stamp designs on frames with inks. Punch holes, place large frame in pan, melt. Stamp mask with Black ink on acetate, insert in melted powder. Add more powder, melt. Sprinkle with beads, insert paper clip. Make hanger and connector with wire and beads. Tie fibers through the opening in small frame. Adhere the feathers.

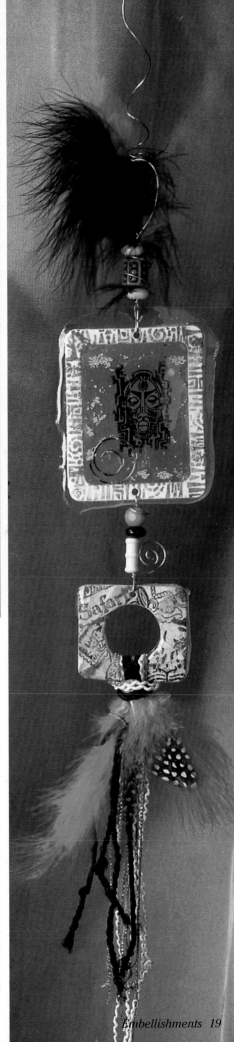

Holiday Cheer

Say thanks with beautiful autumn colors!

Thankful Heart - MATERIALS: 4¼" x 5½" Brown card • Cardstock (4" x 5" piece of Metallic Gold, 4" x 5" piece of Brown, 3½" x 5" piece of Glossy White) • Rubber stamps (Thankful Heart, Small Maple Leaf) • Ancient Page ink (Sage, Gold Encore) • Champagne PEARLustre • 1" Mango sheer ribbon • Gold metallic sheet • Diamond Dot circles • Heat tool • Brayer • Green watercolor pencil • Water Brush • Deckle scissors • Metallic Gold marker • FabriTac
TIPS: Trim Brown cardstock with deckle scissors. Stamp Maple leaf with Sage. Brayer with Sage. Layer cardstock pieces and mount on card. Stamp Thankful Heart and emboss Copper. Add Diamond Dots. Color leaf with pencil and brush. Brayer metallic sheet, mount on card and add ribbon.

Tag Box - MATERIALS: Papier-mâché box • Manila shipping tags • Rubber stamps (Thankful Heart, Harvest Leaf, Harvest Pumpkin, Wire Thank You) • Brilliance ink (Galaxy Gold, Cosmic Copper) • Copper embossing powder • PEARlustre (Champagne, Ruby, Emerald, Amethyst) • 4 large Gold beads • Assorted E beads • Assorted fiber • Heat tool • Round-nose pliers • FabriTac
TIPS: Color box with Brilliance ink. Stamp Wire Thankful heart, emboss Champagne. Stamp remaining designs randomly, emboss as desired. Thread beads on wire, shape. Make holes in lid, insert ends of wire, bend flat on back. Glue beads for feet. Stamp tags and emboss as desired. Tie fibers in holes. Place tags in box.

Wire Thank You - MATERIALS: 5½" square Gold card • White glossy cardstock • Rubber stamps (Wired Leaves, Harvest Leaf, Wire Thank You, Foliate Quad Cube) • Brilliance inks (Galaxy Gold, Cosmic Copper) • Champagne PEARLustre • Copper Embossing powder • Metallic markers (Gold, Copper) • 22 gauge Copper wire • Assorted E beads • Heat tool • Craft knife • ¹⁄₁₆" hole punch • Round-nose pliers • Spray water bottle • Sponge • FabriTac
TIPS: Stamp Foliate Quad Cube on front of card, emboss with Champagne. Place drops of marker inks on cardstock, spray with water, turn from side to side to spread, let dry. Apply Brilliance inks, blend with sponge. Stamp, emboss Copper Wire Thank You Stamp, emboss Copper Wire Leaves and Harvest Leaf around edges. Cut around leaves with craft knife. Punch holes in stems, add wire and beads. Mount panel on card.

Christmas in Green

Send cheerful, colorful greetings to all!

Ornament - MATERIALS: Frosted glass ornament • Ponderosa Pine rubber stamp • Clear embossing ink • Embossing powder (White, Emerald Green) • ¼" Burgundy ribbon • Diamond Dots • Heat tool
TIPS: Stamp, emboss designs. Apply circles, tie ribbon on hanger.

Warm Winter Wishes - MATERIALS: 4¼" x 5½" Green card • Cardstock (White, Burgundy, Green, Metallic Gold) • Rubber stamps (Snowflake Flurry, Prancer, Tiny Trees) • VersaMark ink pads (Watermark, Gold) • PEARLustre (Champagne, Garnet, Emerald) • Gold Ultra Fine glitter • Gold Christmas Messages Class A'Peels • Heat tool • Water Brush • Watercolor pencils • Metallic Gold marker • Mrs. Glue
TIPS: Stamp Gold Snowflake Flurry on card, emboss with Champagne powder. Stamp Prancer on White, emboss Garnet and watercolor. Add glitter to antlers. Layer on Green and Metallic Gold and outline with marker. Stamp Tiny Tree on White, emboss Emerald, watercolor and add glitter to dots. Layer on Metallic Gold and Burgundy, outline with marker. Apply stickers to White, layer on Metallic Gold and Burgundy, outline with marker. Mount panels.

Star Card - MATERIALS: 4¼" x 5½" White glossy card • Green handmade paper • White Mini Matts Geo Frames • Rubber stamps (Wire Star, Ponderosa Pine, Christmas Sentiments) • Ink (Jet Black StazOn, Coal and Pine Ancient Page, Gold VersaMark) • Gold Metallic Sheet • Apple Red and Moss Ultra Fine glitter • 26 gauge Red wire • Assorted beads • Stylus • ⅛" hole punch • Sticky Squares • Glue marker
TIPS: Stamp Ponderosa Pine in Pine ink and Christmas Coal Sentiments on card. Stamp Black Wire Star on back of metallic sheet, trace with stylus, cut out and punch hole in top. Wrap star with wire and beads. Make diagonal strips on frame with glue marker and add Apple Red glitter. Add Moss and Apple Red glitter to holly, berries. Crumple paper, brush with Gold ink and mount on card. Mount frame and star with Sticky Squares.

Tag Card - MATERIALS: 4¼" x 5½" Green card • Cardstock (Red, Green) • 2 White tags • Rubber stamps (Stocking, Candy Cane, Wire Star Border) • Ink (Gold VersaMark, Black ColorBox) • Champagne PEARLustre • Diamond Dot circles • Assorted beads • ¹⁄₁₆" Red ribbon • Gold cord • Green fiber • Corner rounder • Heat tool • Water Brush • Watercolor pencils • Glue
TIPS: Stamp Gold Wire Star Border on card, emboss Champagne. Stamp Black Stocking and Candy Cane on tags, cut bottoms and round corners. Watercolor and apply Diamond Dots. Tie ribbon, cord and fiber on tags, add beads. Mount tags on cardstock and card.

Old Fashioned Ornaments

From Grandma to baby, everyone will love these clever ornaments!

Angel Ornament - MATERIALS: 4 Black Mini Matts Ovals • Angelica rubber stamp • Clear embossing ink • Gold Tinsel embossing powder • Gold double tassel • Metallic markers (Gold, Green, Blue, Purple) • Heat tool • FabriTac

TIPS: Stamp and emboss Angelica on ovals. Paint with markers. Score through centers of ovals with craft knife before gently bending at a 90° angle. Glue ovals together sandwiching tassel. Outline edges with Gold marker.

Poinsettia Ornament - MATERIALS: 4 White Mini Matts Ovals • Rubber stamps (Poinsettia Points, Faux Finish Quad Cube) • Gold Brilliance ink • Clear embossing ink • Gold Tinsel embossing powder • Gold double tassel • Water Brush • Watercolor pencils • Heat tool • FabriTac

TIPS: Stamp Gold background on ovals. Stamp and emboss Poinsettia Points. Watercolor. Score through centers of ovals with craft knife before gently bending at a 90° angle. Glue ovals together sandwiching tassel.

Christmas in Blue

Shimmering blue and silver light the way to a season of hope and cheer!

Blue Ornament - MATERIALS: Frosted ornament • Clear embossing ink • Embossing powder (Sterling Silver, Kaleidoscope) • 1½" Silver ribbon • Heat tool

TIPS: Cover ornament and top with ink, emboss using both colors. Tie ribbon on hanger.

Blessed Night Card - MATERIALS: 5½" square Ivory card • 3 Black Retro Mini Matts • Black cardstock • Blessed Night rubber stamp • Brilliance ink (Mediterranean Blue, Platinum Planet, Pearlescent Purple, Cosmic Copper, Pearlescent Ice Blue, Moonlight White) • Cobalt Blue embossing powder • Fibers • Heat tool • Sponge • FabriTac

TIPS: Apply Moonlight White ink to card. Stroke Mediterranean Blue with sponge. Stamp Platinum Planet Blessed Night in corners. Stamp on cardstock, emboss Cobalt. Tear into 2 pieces and mount on card. Place Mini Matts together, stamp and emboss Cobalt Blue. Color with Brilliance ink. Heat set ink and mount. Tie fibers around card.

Sparkling Radiance Card - MATERIALS: 4¼" x 5½" White glossy card • Rubber stamps (Season Bright, Snowflake Flurry, Small Wire Snowflake, Snow Swirl, Large Wire Snowflake) • Pearlescent Brilliance re-inkers (Sky Blue, Jade, Lavender, Mediterranean Blue) • VersaMark Ink (Silver, Blue) • PEARLustre (Sterling Silver, Sapphire) • Diamond Dots • Metallic cord • Assorted beads • Hexagon template • Heat tool • Cutting mat • Swivel craft knife • Talcum powder

TIPS: Brush Brilliance re-inkers on card. Cut window using template. Stamp Silver Small Wire Snowflake, emboss Sapphire. Rub powder on front of card, stamp remaining designs with Silver, emboss Sterling Silver. Add Diamond Dots. Tie fibers around card and add beads.

Snowman Card - MATERIALS: 4⅝" x 5⅞" Blue card • Cardstock (Metallic Silver, Blue, White) • Rubber stamps (Snow Boy, Small Wire Snowflake) • Cerulean ColorBox ink • Clear embossing powder • Silver Class A'Peels stickers (Merry Christmas, seals) • Diamond Dot circles • Water Brush • Watercolor pencils • Double-sided adhesive • Sticky Dots

TIPS: Stamp Cerulean Snow Boy on White, emboss with Clear, watercolor. Apply seals to corners, Diamond Dots to Snow Boy. Layer on Blue and Metallic Silver. Place double sided adhesive on White cardstock, crumple foil and place flat on double-sided adhesive and remove. Stamp Cerulean Small Wire Snowflake. Cover cardstock with Clear powder and emboss. Mount pieces on card, add sticker.

Tag - MATERIALS: White tag • Rubber stamps (Snow Swirl, Snowflake Flurry) • Subtle Crafters ink • Clear Embossing ink • Embossing powder (Silver Tinsel, Sterling Silver) • Alphabet Script Class A'Peels • White and Silver fiber • Diamond Dots • Heat tool

TIPS: Color tag with Crafters ink. Stamp Snowflake Flurry, emboss Silver Tinsel. Stamp Snow Swirl, emboss Sterling Silver. Apply Diamond Dots and tie fibers on tag.

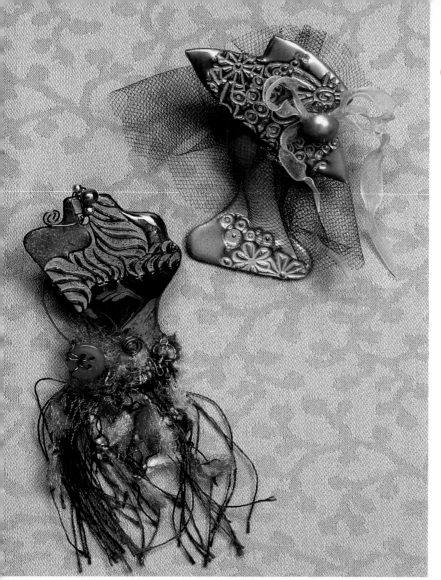

Deep Impressions
with

PEARLustre
EMBOSSING POWDER

Jewelry with a lustrous finish makes a perfect gift for the lady whose closet is filled with the latest fashions!

Fringed Torso - MATERIALS: Millinery Mini Matts • Prancing Zebra rubber stamp • Deep Impression Clear embossing powder • PEARLustre embossing powders (Garnet, Amethyst, Champagne) • Silver pigment ink • Button • 26 gauge Green wire • Beads
TIPS: Punch holes in top and bottom of matt, place in pan, spoon Clear powder over piece and melt. Sprinkle with various embossing powders and melt. Swirl colors together. Remove and stamp. Clean holes and edges. Embellish with fibers, button, wire and beads. Adhere pin back.

Sunday Best Pin - MATERIALS: White Millinery Mini Matts • Millefiori Vase rubber stamp • Deep Impression Clear embossing powder • Silver embossing powder • PEARLustre (Tanzanite, Rose Quartz, Alexandrite) • Silver pigment ink • 1/4" Pink sheer ribbon • Black tulle circle • Pearl button • Heat tool
TIPS: Place pieces in pan, spoon on Clear powder and melt. Sprinkle with PEARLustre, melt. Swirl colors together. Remove and stamp. Clean holes and edges. Adhere tulle between hat and head shape. Attach ribbon bow and curl by applying heat tool carefully. Adhere pearl button, pin back.

MATERIALS: Mini Matts • Deep Impression Clear embossing powder • Pin back • Craft pan • Hot Sheet • Round-nose pliers • 1/8" hole punch • Stylus • FabriTac

1. Select mini matts shape and punch holes.

2. Place on Hot Sheet in pan heated to 300°F and spoon on Deep Impression powder.

3. Sprinkle PEARLustre powders over melted powder, melt.

4. Use stylus to swirl colors. Remove Hot Sheet from pan. Slide piece slightly to aid in edge cleaning.

5. With pre-inked rubber stamp, stamp design while still hot. Cool before removing. Clean holes.

6. Clean the edges on a Hot Sheet in pan.

7. Add wire and bead embellishments and jewelry findings.

Moroccan Screen Book - MATERIALS: Black Mini Matts Squares • Morrocan Screen rubber stamp • Gold Encore ink • Deep Impression Clear embossing powder • Verdigris embossing powder • 72" of Gold cord • Assorted beads
TIPS: Punch holes in 2 matts. Place in pan. Sprinkle with Clear powder and melt. Sprinkle with Verdigris, melt. Ink stamp, remove matt and immediately impress image leaving rubber stamp embedded until cool. Remove stamp and smooth edges on Hot Sheet in pan. Clean holes. Cut or tear pieces of handmade paper to fit inside covers. Punch holes in side edges. Layer pieces and stitch book together wrapping each hole at a diagonal down spine and bringing back up again the opposite to form X's up spine. Knot at top and add beads and knots up sides of cord as desired. Knot ends together.

Accordion Book - MATERIALS: White Mini Matts Geo Frames • Thermo Acetate • Cardstock • Rubber stamps (Floral Tile, Laurel Leaf Border, Words of Friendship) • Clear ink • Brilliance ink (Pearlescent Orchid, Gamma Green, Cosmic Copper) • Deep Impression Clear embossing powder • PEARLustre (Carnelian, Adventurine, Tanzanite) • Photos • Metallic Rub-Ons • Gold Victorian Borders Class A'Peels • Elastic cord • Green and Gold beads • Gold shank button • Stipple brush • Glue sticks
TIPS: Punch hole on right center edge of front cover. Place pieces in pan, spoon Clear powder over pieces, melt. Sprinkle with PEARLustre powders, melt. Pre-ink stamp with Clear ink, clean edges, remove and immediately stamp images. Let cool before removing stamp. Clean holes. Adhere acetate piece behind front cover. Fold cardstock accordion style into 2¼" x 2¾" booklet. Stamp images as desired on pages. Stipple pages with inks to age. Glue booklet in covers leaving open at top of front cover for photo. Insert shanked button through hole. Fold cord in half and tie knot in end leaving 2" tail. Insert folded end through shank, tying knot after shank. Loop around book and attach over button in front for closure. Mount photos stickers. Insert photo in front cover.

Retro Swirl - MATERIALS: Black Retro Mini Matts • Tiled Quad Cube rubber stamp • Copper Brilliance ink • Deep Impression Clear embossing powder • PEARLustre (Sapphire, Carnelian) • Hair pick comb with wire prongs • Assorted beads • 26 gauge Blue wire • Spatula
TIPS: Punch holes in matt, place in pan, spoon Clear powder over piece and melt. Sprinkle with PEARLustre, melt. Use comb to swirl colors. Clean edges. Pre-ink stamp, remove, stamp image and let cool before removing stamp. Repeat with smaller image. Clean holes. Embellish with wire and beads. Adhere pin back.

Zig Zag Purse Pin - MATERIALS: Black Retro Mini Matts • Zig Zag Border rubber stamp • Gold pigment ink • Deep Impression Clear embossing powder • PEARLustre (Ruby, Champagne) • 24 gauge Gold wire • Tiny beads • ⅞" Gold sheer ribbon • Pin back
TIPS: Punch holes in matt, place in pan, spoon Clear powder over piece, melt. Sprinkle with PEARLustre, melt. Pre-ink stamp, remove from pan, immediately stamp image. Let cool before removing stamp. Clean holes. Embellish with wire handle, bead, ribbon.

Butterfly Pin - MATERIALS: Retro Mini Matts • Flutterby rubber stamp • Deep Impression Clear embossing powder • Gold pigment ink • PEARLustre (Carnelian, Tanzanite, Rose Quartz) • 26 gauge Blue wire • Assorted beads • Pin back
TIPS: Punch holes in matt, place in pan, spoon Clear powder over piece and melt. Sprinkle with PEARLustre, melt. Pre-ink stamp, remove from pan. Immediately stamp image. Let cool before removing stamp. Clean holes. Embellish with wire and beads.

Grande Soiree Purse Pin - MATERIALS: Rectangle Mini Matts • Grande Soiree rubber stamp • Gold pigment ink • Deep Impression Clear embossing powder • Champagne PEARLustre • 24 gauge Gold wire • Button • Gold bead • Pin back
TIPS: Punch holes in matt shape, place in pan, spoon Clear powder over piece, melt. Sprinkle with PEARLustre, melt. Pre-ink stamp, remove, immediately stamp image. Let cool before removing. Clean holes. Embellish with wire handle, button, bead.

more Great Ideas on the following pages!

Holiday Decor
with

Ornaments, bows and cards embossed with metallic colors bring extra special sparkle to your festive holidays!

PEARLustre
EMBOSSING POWDER

1. Cover ornament with Clear embossing ink.

2. Sprinkle with embossing powder and heat.

Ornament with Ribbon - MATERIALS: Glass ornaments • Clear embossing ink • PEARLustre (Champagne, Emerald, Garnet) • Multi Ultra Fine glitter • 1½" striped ribbon
TIPS: Cover ornament with Clear ink, sprinkle with embossing powder and heat. Sprinkle with glitter while still melted. Tie ribbon on hanger.

Bow - MATERIALS: Ribbon (2½" White satin with Gold wire edge, 1½" Burgundy, ¼" Burgundy) • Rubber stamps (Wire Star, Wire Poinsettia) • Clear embossing ink • Champagne PEARlustre
TIPS: Stamp White ribbon with Wire Star and emboss. Stamp and emboss 1½" Burgundy ribbon with Wire Poinsettia. Make bow with each wide ribbon and tie together with ¼" ribbon.

Card - MATERIALS: 4¼" x 5½" Beige card • 5½" x 8½" piece of Pastel Yellow vellum • Rubber stamps (Classic Plume, Champagne, Classic Roses) • Brown ink • Deep Impression Clear embossing ink • Champagne PEARLustre • Decorative scissors • Punches (1/16" circle, ¼" heart) • 1" Moss Green sheer ribbon • Colored pencils (Green, Red, White, Blue, Yellow)
TIPS: Fold vellum in half and cut point with decorative scissors. Punch edge. Stamp with Clear Classic Plume and emboss Champagne. Stamp Brown Classic Roses on card and color. Stamp with Clear Classic Plume and emboss Champagne. Layer, punch hearts in fold and tie together with ribbon.

Ornament - MATERIALS: Glass ornaments • Clear embossing ink • PEARlustre (Champagne, Amethyst, Carnelian)
TIPS: Cover ornament with Clear ink, sprinkle with embossing powder and heat.

Gift - MATERIALS: White gift wrap • ⅜" Burgundy satin with Gold edge ribbon • Gold pearl garland • White paper wrapped wire • Wire Poinsettia rubber stamp • Red and Green ink • Champagne PEARlustre • Sponge
TIPS: Stamp gift wrap with Green Wire Poinsettias. Sponge with Red ink. Sprinkle with Champagne, emboss. Tie bow, add garland, wire.

Never send an ordinary card, send one filled with color and texture and say, "I made it myself!"

1. Stamp background with Gold ink and emboss with Champagne PEARLustre.

2. Melt leftover puddles of embossing powder with heat tool.

3. Add mesh scraps and ribbons to puddles and insert Mini Matt shape. Add more puddles and melt.

4. Ink stamp and press design into puddle. Let cool.

Window on Africa Card - MATERIALS: Retro Mini Matts Frame • Square glossy Black card • Rubber stamps (Giraffes, Palm Fronds, Zig Zag Border) • Gold pigment ink • PEARLustre embossing powders (Carnelian, Champagne, Adventurine, Rose Quartz) • Magic Mesh scrap • 24 gauge Gold wire • Assorted seed beads • Heat tool • Hot Sheet • 1/16" hole punch • Round-nose pliers
TIPS: Place frame on Hot Sheet, spoon with Clear powder and melt. Melt puddles of PEARLustre over frame. Pre-ink Giraffes stamp. Immediately stamp image. Let cool before removing stamp. Stamp images on card and emboss with PEARLustre powders. Sprinkle extra powder on card and melt with heat tool. Stick mesh scrap on card. Punch holes and use wire to attach frame to card, coil wire at ends and add beads

Puddled Impressions - MATERIALS: Long Pewter card • Artistic Impressions wood rubber stamp set • Clear and Silver ink • Deep Impression Clear embossing powder • Moonstone PEARLustre • Left over puddles of melted PEARLustre • Ribbon (Moss, Frost, Eggplant) • Magic Mesh scrap • Metallic Copper marker • Heat tool • Hot Sheet
TIPS: Stamp background with Clear ink and emboss with Moonstone. Brush edges of card with Clear ink pad and emboss. Place several puddles on card and melt with heat tool. Place ribbons and mesh scrap in puddles. Add more puddles and stamp pre-inked design into puddles. Let cool.

Snakeskin Shoe - MATERIALS: Fan Mini Matts shape • Matte White high heel card • Rubber stamps (Snakeskin, Stitched Scallop) • Clear and Gold pigment inks • Deep Impression Clear embossing powder • PEARLustre (Champagne, Tanzanite, Hessonite, Peridot) • Black tulle circle • 22 gauge Gold wire • Craft pan • Heat tool • Hot Sheet • Wire tool • FabriTac
TIPS: Stamp design on shoe with Clear ink and emboss with various PEARLustre powders. Place matt shape on Hot Sheet in pan at 300°. Spoon Clear powder over piece and melt. Sprinkle with PEARLustre powders and melt. Pre-ink stamp. Remove Hot Sheet from pan and immediately stamp image. Let cool before removing stamp. Clean edges on Hot Sheet in pan. Gather 1/4 of tulle circle and adhere to shoe. Layer coiled wire and Deep Impression piece on top.

Album Stand - MATERIALS: Album stand with wood cover • Rubber stamps (Classic Plume, Foliate Quad Cube) • Black StazOn ink • Ancient Page Coal ink • Clear Embossing Ink • Deep Impression Clear embossing powder • Metallic Sheet • Rub-Ons (Gold, Green) • Acrylic paint (Pink, Moss Green, Black) • Heat tool • Sponge brush • Black pen • FabriTac • Terry cloth

TIPS: Paint cover in Black acrylic. Stamp Foliate Quad Cube in Clear embossing ink. Dust with Clear embossing powder. Heat. Paint Pink and rub off embossed areas. Stamp metallic sheet with Classic Plume and emboss with stylus. Cut out and glue in center of cover. Paint opening Moss Green and write title. Sponge metal and title with Black. Apply Rub-Ons to metal and title.

White Box - MATERIALS: Wood box with drawer • Rubber stamps (Foliate Quad Cube, Shell Plaque, Blossom Plaque) • Clear embossing ink • Champagne PEARLustre • Wood bead • Class A'Peels Gold numbers and letters • White paper • White acrylic paint • Heat tool • Sponge brush • Sticky Squares • FabriTac • Terry cloth

TIPS: Stamp box with Foliate Quad Cube and emboss Champagne. Paint box and bead White, rub paint off embossed areas on box. Rub edges with ink pad, sprinkle with Champagne and emboss. Stamp frame and tag on metallic sheet, emboss with stylus and cut out. Cut paper to fit behind frame, apply message stickers and mount frame with tape. Apply number stickers to tag, mount and glue bead for handle.

Candle - MATERIALS: White pillar candle • Deep Rose Border rubber stamp • Black StazOn ink • Metallic sheet • Gold brads • 2 straight pins

TIPS: Stamp metallic sheet, emboss with stylus and cut out. Wrap around candle and attach in back with straight pins. Randomly attach brads.

Antiqued Box - MATERIALS: Wood box • Rubber Stamps (Tiled Quad Cube, Foliate Cube) • Black StazOn ink • Clear embossing ink • Deep Impression Clear embossing powder • Copper metallic sheet • Copper Rub-Ons • Russet and Ivory acrylic paints • Heat tool • Paintbrush • FabriTac • Terry cloth

TIPS: Paint box Russet, let dry. Stamp Tiled Quad Cube on box with Clear ink and emboss with Clear powder. Paint box Ivory, let dry. Remove paint from embossed areas with damp terry cloth. Stamp Foliate Cube on metallic sheet cut to fit front of box, emboss with stylus and rub with ink. Adhere to front of box with FabriTac. Stamp Tiled Quad Cube on metallic square, emboss, ink and adhere to top of box. Apply Rub-Ons for aging and highlights.

Metal Plaque Card - MATERIALS: 5½" square Black glossy card • Ivory cardstock • Rubber stamps (Shell Plaque, Foliate Cube) • Black permanent ink • Gold pigment ink • Deep Impression Clear embossing powder • Gold metallic sheet • Class A'Peels letters • 1" Sage Green sheer ribbon • Sage acrylic paint • Gold Rub-Ons • ¼" hole punch • Sticky squares • Gold marker • Paper towel

TIPS: Stamp Foliate Cube on front of card with Gold ink and emboss with Clear powder. Paint with Sage and let air dry. Scrub paint off of embossed areas with damp towel. Enhance with Rub-Ons. Stamp Shell Plaque on metallic sheet with Black permanent ink, emboss with stylus and cut out. Apply stickers to Ivory cardstock and cut to fit frame. Layer frame over saying and secure with sticky squares. Embellish with ribbon and outline edge with marker.

MATERIALS: Black StazOn ink • Foam mat • Stylus • Scissors • Sponge

1. Stamp design on back of metallic sheet with StazOn ink.

2. Place on foam mat. Emboss design with stylus.

3. Sponge the ink on the front of raised image.

4. Cut out the design and mount as desired.

Shoe Card - MATERIALS: Matte White high heel card • Rubber stamps (Wire Poinsettia, Merry Christmas) • Black ink • Clear embossing ink • Black embossing powder • Gold metallic sheet • Diamond Dots • Itty Bitty Gold beads • Punches (1/16" circle, 1/8" circle, teardrop) • Decorative scissors • Colored pencils • Double-sided adhesive sheet • FabriTac

TIPS: Stamp Black Wire Poinsettia on card and color with pencils. Apply Diamond Dots. Apply beads to bow pieces with double-sided adhesive. Cut 5½" square of metallic sheet with decorative scissor and punch design around the edges. Stamp Clear Merry Christmas and emboss Black. Glue the card on metallic piece and bow on shoe.

Dress Ornament - MATERIALS: Gown of Dreams rubber stamp • Black StazOn ink • Filigree Class A'Peels border • Silver Diamond Dots • Gold metallic sheet • 1/8" hole punch • Tinsel cord • Fibers • Pearl spray • Sponge

TIPS: Stamp design on metallic sheet, emboss with stylus and cut out. Sponge ink lightly over raised image. Apply stickers and Diamond Dots. Trace the border with a stylus. Punch a hole and attach the embellishments.

Red Tin - MATERIALS: 3" metal tin • Rubber stamps (Tiled Quad Cube, Faux Finish Quad Cube) • Clear embossing ink • Black Staz-On ink • Champagne PEARLustre • Burgundy acrylic paint • Paintbrush • FabriTac

TIPS: Paint tin Burgundy, let dry. Stamp Clear Faux Finish Quad Cube and emboss Champagne. Stamp Tiled Quad Cube on metallic sheet, emboss with stylus and cut out. Sponge ink lightly over raised image. Glue metallic square on lid.

STAMPENDOUS!®
impressions every time

Magic on Metal

Antiqued or shiny bright, you'll love to rubber stamp and emboss images on metal!

Breezy Flight Card - MATERIALS: Cardstock (5½" and 2½" squares of Orange, 4¼" x 5½" piece of Yellow, 1¼" x 5½" piece and 2½" square of Light Orange) • Rubber stamps (Dragonfly Points, Breezy Flight) • Inks (Coal, Sandalwood, Mandarin, Saffron) • Tan yarn • Gold pony bead • 2½" Gold metallic sheet • ¼" hole punch • Heat tool • Deckle scissors • Sponge • FabriTac

TIPS: Stamp Dragonfly Points on metal piece, emboss and create hammered edge with stylus. Trim with deckle scissors. Stamp Dragonfly Points softly on Yellow cardstock with Mandarin ink. Sponge other inks on remaining cardstock pieces. Glue Light Orange cardstock on left side. Fold Orange cardstock over edge of Yellow and adhere. Stamp Breezy Flight with Coal ink. Punch hole in side and add yarn and bead tie. Layer metal square over Orange squares and adhere.

Hammered Copper Dragonfly Card - MATERIALS: Sage notecard • White mulberry paper scrap • Rubber stamps (Ma Dragonfly, Sunshine Wave, Petite Dragonfly) • Black StazOn ink • Sage Ancient Page ink • Copper and Silver pigment inks • Deep Impression Clear embossing powder • 3" square of Copper metallic sheet • Silk leaf • Metallic Copper marker • FabriTac

TIPS: Stamp Ma Dragonfly on metallic sheet, emboss and cut out. Trim with deckle scissors. Stamp other images randomly on card with Versamark ink. Sponge border of various inks and emboss. Follow same steps on leaf. Glue pieces on card.

Christmas Page - MATERIALS: Mini Matts shapes • Cardstock (Green, White, Red) • Rubber stamps (Faux Finish Quad Cube, Artiste Quad Cube, Wired Holly Ball, Retro Ornaments, Christmas Gift, Love Gift, Ponderosa Pine, Christmas Sentiments, Candy Cane, Stocking) • Ink (Red, Green, Clear embossing) • Champagne PEARLustre • Class A'Peels (Circle Medallions, Holiday Trends Border, Letters, Numbers) • Gold star brad • 24 Gauge Gold wire • 2 Red beads • ¼" sheer ribbon (Green, Dark Green, Red) • Gold cord • Red marker

Fall Heritage Page - MATERIALS: Cardstock (Wine, Tan) • Banana vellum • Rubber stamps (Foliate Quad Cube, Laurel Leaf Border) • Ancient Page ink (Sage, Plum Wine) • Class A'Peel (Letters, Leaves) • Metallic E beads • ¼" Moss ribbon • Sticky Squares

Dragonfly Candle - MATERIALS: Ivory pillar candle • Ivory mulberry paper • Silver Dragonfly Border Class A'Peels • Multi Ultra Fine glitter • ⅞" Lavender sheer ribbon • Heat tool • Paintbrush • Permanent markers • Glue
TIPS: Apply Dragonfly border to mulberry paper Color with markers. Apply glue, sprinkle with glitter. Let dry. Soften sides of candle with heat tool. Apply paper to candle, reheating as necessary to attach. Apply negative portions of flowers. Tie ribbon around candle, use heat tool to curl.

Leaves Page - MATERIALS: Black Mini Matts Oval • Cardstock (Teal, Parchment, Wine) • Vellum (Pale Blueberry, Banana) • Vellum envelope • Rubber stamps (Floral Tile, Laurel Leaf Border) • Ancient Page ink (Deep Harbor, Plum Wine, Brocade Silk) • Deep Impression Clear embossing powder • Copper embossing powder • Class A'Peels (Leaves, Eyelets, Brads, Numbers) • Silk leaves • Punches (⅛" circle, corner rounder) • Sticky Squares • Deckle scissors

Notepad - MATERIALS: 4¼" x 5½" notepad • Cardstock (Kraft, White) • Metallic paper (Gold, Copper) • Tiled Quad Cube rubber stamp • VersaColor ink (Khaki, Copper) • Deep Impression Clear embossing ink • Champagne PEARLustre • Vintage Chain Class A'Peels • Deckle scissors • FabriTac
TIPS: For cover, cut Kraft cardstock slightly larger than notepad. Ink stamp with Khaki and Copper and stamp front of cover. Stamp Tiled Quad on Kraft and cut out with deckle scissors. Stamp and emboss on White, cut out with deckle scissors. Layer and glue on metallic squares trimmed slightly larger than stamped squares. Glue on the cover. Cut 3" strip of Gold paper the width of cover, trim one edge with deckle scissors, fold and glue for spine. Apply the stickers.

Mother's Day Card - MATERIALS: 4¼" x 5½" Black notecard • Cardstock (2" and 2½" squares of Black glossy, 4" x 5¼" piece of White) • Happy Mother's Day rubber stamp • Gold Class A'Peels (Square Frames, Oval Border, Gold Rose For You) • Metallic Green pigment ink • Pigment inks (Sky Blue, Pink, Heliotrope, Mint) • Paintbrush • Watercolor pencils • Metallic Pink and Metallic Green markers • Water in fine spray bottle • Plastic wrap • Sponge • Glue
TIPS: Spray fine mist on Black glossy squares, make several drops of marker ink on misted cardstock, crumple plastic wrap and set on top of squares. Remove plastic when dry. Sponge inks on White cardstock. Apply square stickers to cardstock squares. Apply rose to White cardstock scrap, watercolor and cut out. Stamp saying with Metallic Green ink. Layer all elements on card. Embellish with border stickers.

Father's Day Card - MATERIALS: 4¼" x 5½" Brown note card • Brown and Gold corrugated paper • 4" x 5¼" piece of Parchment cardstock • Alphabet stamp set • Ink (Brown, Old Rose, Gold) • Gold Masculine Group Shirts Class A'Peels • Watercolor pencils • Paintbrush • Diamond pattern stencil • Sponge • Tape • Glue
TIPS: Apply positive image of shirt to cardstock. Apply tape to negative image and remove from sheet. Apply to cardstock. Watercolor and cut out. Mount on trimmed corrugated paper. Use inks to stencil pattern on Parchment panel. Stamp words with Brown ink. Adhere all pieces to card.

Thinking of You - MATERIALS: Mini Matts Square • 4¼" x 5½" White matte note card • Black Cherry vellum • Class A'Peels (Gold Aloha Border, Gold Sailboat saying) • Pigment ink (Copper, Gold, Silver) • Copper and Silver embossing powders • Gold and Silver tinsel cord • Watercolor pencils • Paintbrush • Heat tool • Sponge
TIPS: Apply Aloha Border to card. Trim along edge. Watercolor inside designs. Sponge inks over card and sprinkle with embossing powders and heat to emboss. Follow same instructions on matt. Punch hole and attach at side of card with cord. Adhere negative image from flowers to matt. Apply saying to card front. Adhere vellum to inside of card even with bottom edge.

Class A'Peels™ Sticker Embellishments

Add intricate designs and elegant lettering to cards and candles in seconds with metallic Class A'Peels stickers!

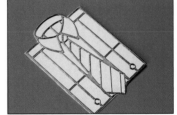

1. Apply positive image from sticker sheet to cardstock.

2. Place strip of tape over negative image, burnish well and remove from carrier sheet.

3. Apply to cardstock, burnish again and remove tape strips.

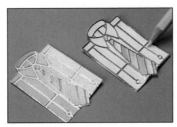

4. Watercolor and cut out.

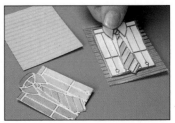

5. Mount on card.

Glass Glitter Ornaments

Turn inexpensive clear balls into classy artistic ornaments with glitter!

Candy Cane Ornament - MATERIALS: Glass ornament • Glitter (Red, Crystal) • 3/8" Red sheer ribbon • Mrs. Glue

Red & Green Ornament - MATERIALS: Glass ornament • Glitter (Red, Green) • Geo Link Border Class A'Peels • Diamond Dots • 3/8" Red sheer ribbon • Double-sided adhesive
TIPS: Cut mosaic shapes from adhesive, apply to ornament and cover with glitter.

Swirl Ornament - MATERIALS: Glass ornament • Glitter (Green, Copper) • 3/8" Red sheer ribbon • Mrs. Glue
TIPS: Coat inside of ornament with glue, add Green glitter, shake to cover and pour out excess. Make glue swirls on outside and sprinkle with Copper.

Mosaic Ornament - MATERIALS: Glass ornament • Glitter (Silver, Red, Gold) • 3/8" Red sheer ribbon • Double-sided adhesive
TIPS: Coat sheet of plastic wrap with Mrs. Glue. Pour glitter colors in bands and let dry 24 hours. Cut into pieces and apply with thinned Mrs. Glue (half glue and half water).

Blue & Gold Ornament - MATERIALS: Frosted glass ornament •Faux Finish Quad Cube • Clear embossing ink • Clear embossing powder • Glitter (Blue, Gold) • Diamond dots • Double sided adhesive • Heat tool• Glue
TIPS: Stamp and emboss design on ornament. Make scallops with glue around top of ornament, apply glitter and let dry. Cut shapes from double-sided adhesive and apply glitter as shown, attach to ornament. Coat cap with glue and apply Blue glitter.

Snow Capped Ornament - MATERIALS: Glass ornament • Glitter (Blue, Silver, Multi) • Snowtex • Pearls by the yard • White tulle • Double-sided adhesive • Glue
TIPS: Coat inside of ornament with glue, add Blue and Silver glitter, shake and pour out excess glitter. Apply glue and Blue glitter to cap. Apply glue and Snowtex. Sprinkle with Multi glitter while still wet. Tie pearls and tulle on hanger

Indoor Garden ~ Glitter Bugs

Turn mini matts, glitter and wire into a bunch of friendly bugs for your indoor garden!

1. Punch holes in shape.

2. Brush on glue then apply the glitter. Let dry, shake off excess.

3. Attach wire and embellish with beads and wiggle eyes.

Exotic Butterfly with Flowerpot - MATERIALS:
Retro Mini Matts • Black dye ink • Glitter (Black, Orange, Yellow Pearl) • Copper and Black Jewel glitter • 20 gauge Copper wire • Black pony beads • 15" of 1/8" diameter dowel • Rose pot • Moss • Styrofoam cone • Raffia • Paintbrush • 1/8" hole punch • Mrs. Glue
TIPS: Apply glue to rim of pot in tiger stripe pattern. Apply glitter Copper and Black. Let dry. Cut foam to fit in pot. Attach raffia bow. Punch holes in wing shapes. Apply glue and glitter to wings alternating glitter colors to form spots. Edge wings with Black glitter, let dry. Attach wings and make bead with wire. Attach to dowel dyed with Black ink. Insert in pot and glue moss as filler.

Bee-Dazzled Bee Photo Clip - MATERIALS:
Black Mini Matts shapes • Wood block • Tiled Quad Cube rubber stamp • Top Boss Clear embossing ink • Deep Impression Clear embossing powder • Black and Yellow acrylic paints • Black and Gold Fine Jewel glitters • Black tulle circle • 22 gauge Silver wire • Alligator clip • Two 4mm wiggle eyes • 1/8" diameter dowel • Paintbrush • 1/16" hole punch • Heat tool • Craft drill and 1/8" bit • Chalk • Mrs. Glue • FabriTac • Terry cloth
TIPS: Drill hole in top of block. Apply Black paint to block and dowel, let dry. Stamp design with Clear ink and emboss with Clear powder. Paint block Yellow, let dry. Gently scrub paint from embossed areas with damp cloth. Apply chalk. Punch holes in matt shapes. Apply glue with brush and sprinkle with glitter, let dry. Glue on eyes. Use wire to attach head to body, sandwiching gathered piece of tulle between layers for wings. Attach bee to dowel with wire and glue. Attach alligator clip with FabriTac. Insert dowel in block and adhere with FabriTac.

Sparkling Dragonfly - MATERIALS:
Black Mini Matts Ovals • Mint Pastel Ultra Fine glitter • 22 gauge Copper wire • Green plastic wire • 8 glass beads • Round-nose pliers • 1/8" hole punch • Mrs. Glue
TIPS: Punch holes in matt shapes. Coat with glue and sprinkle with glitter. Let dry. Attach wings with Green wire. Cut 2 Copper wires 18" long. Spiral ends, twist twice and insert through largest bead. Slip remaining beads over one wire and use other wire to coil around each bead and through wired wing section. Continue to last bead before cutting off excess. Spiral other wire end for tail.

Black Widow - MATERIALS:
Black Mini Matts Circles • Red and Black fine Jewel glitter • 20 gauge Black wire • Paintbrush • 1/8" hole punch • Round-nose pliers • Two 4mm wiggle eyes • Mrs. Glue
TIPS: Punch holes for legs and attaching body to head. Apply hourglass shaped of spot glue on large circle. Coat with Red glitter. Coat head with glue and add Black glitter. Let dry. Apply glue and Black glitter to remainder of body, let dry. Attach head to body with 8" of wire, twist and shape antennae. Attach legs by inserting one 6" piece of wire through 2 leg openings before spiraling ends. Adhere eyes with glue and let dry.

Lady Glitterbug - MATERIALS:
Black Mini Matts Circles • Red and Black fine Jewel glitter • 18 gauge Red and Black wire • Two 4mm wiggle eyes • Paintbrush • 1/8" hole punch • Round-nose pliers • Mrs. Glue
TIPS: Punch holes for legs and attaching body to head. Apply spots of glue on large circle. Coat with Black glitter. Coat head with glue and Black glitter. Let dry. Apply glue and Red glitter to remainder of body, let dry. Attach head to body with 8" of Red wire, twist and shape antennae. Attach legs by inserting piece of Black wire through 2 leg openings before spiraling ends. Adhere eyes with glue, let dry.

Fly Swatter - MATERIALS:
Mini Matts (Black Geo Frame, Black Oval, White Oval) • Multi Ultra Fine Crystal glitter • Fine Jewel glitter (Royal, Emerald, Black) • Black Magic Mesh • Wire (22 gauge Silver, 22 gauge Purple, 20 gauge galvanized) • 7/8" Teal sheer ribbon • 2 pairs of 4mm wiggle eyes • Mrs. Glue
TIPS: Punch holes for antennae and attaching wings to body. Brush wings with glue and sprinkle with Multi glitter. Brush body with glue and apply Royal and Emerald glitter, let dry. Cut mesh to fit inside 2 frame matts. Coat matts with glue and apply Black glitter, let dry. Secure mesh between frames. Form galvanized wire handle around frame. Attach wings and one body with Silver wire, glue on front of swatter. Attach other fly pieces to back with Purple wire. Adhere eyes with glue. Tie ribbon around handle.

Botanica
COLLECTION™

Botanical

Give cards and pins with a botanical theme to all the avid gardeners on your list!

Royal Orchid Pin - MATERIALS: White Mini Matts • Rubber stamps (Royal Orchid Script, Leopard Texture Cube) • Ink (Blue, Brown) • Deep Impression Clear embossing powder • PEARLustre (Ruby, Carnelian) • Assorted beads • 24 gauge Burgundy wire • 1/8" hole punch • Round-nose pliers • Hot Sheet • Craft pan • Metallic Copper marker • Colored pencils
TIPS: Punch holes in matts and stamp with Blue Royal Orchid Script and Brown Leopard Texture Cube. Color orchid with pencils. Place on Hot Sheet in pan heated to 300°F, sprinkle with Clear powder and melt. Sprinkle with PEARLustre, melt. Attach mats with wire and beads. Outline with marker. Adhere pin back.

Vesta Orchid Pin - MATERIALS: Black Retro Mini Matts • Vesta Orchid rubber stamp • Clear embossing ink • Yellow embossing powder • Acrylic paints (Burgundy, Teal, Green, Orange) • 22 gauge wire (Gold Orange) • Assorted beads • Leopard button • Pin back • Paintbrush • 1/8" hole punch • Heat tool • Metallic Gold marker • FabriTac • Terry cloth
TIPS: Stamp design with Clear and emboss Yellow. Apply paints to design. Let dry. Gently scrub paint from embossed areas with damp terry cloth. Finish edges with marker. Punch holes. Push shank of button through hole and add coiled wire accent. Embellish at bottom with dangles of spiraled wire and beads. Adhere pin back.

Jungle Botanica Card - MATERIALS: Mini Matts (White Triangle, Black Geo Frame) • White matte long card • Rubber stamps (Purebeck Gold Orchid, Royal Orchid Script, Mini Moth, Vesta Orchid, Primitive Fringe, Zebra Stripes, Textile Border) • Clear embossing ink • Ancient Page inks (Pine, Foxglove, Primrose, Coal) • Vivid Yellow and Cobalt embossing powders • Tassel • Clear Itty Bitty Beads • Dimensional Magic • Postage stamp • Acrylic paints (Yellow, Lavender, Blue Red) • Paintbrush • 1/8" hole punch • Heat tool • Watercolor pencils • FabriTac
TIPS: Stamp designs on card front in various inks. Color with pencils. Tear right edge. Stamp Zebra Stripes with Coal ink along inside edge. Stamp designs on Mini Matt shapes with Clear ink. Emboss frame with Vivid Yellow and triangle piece with Cobalt. Apply paints to triangle piece, let dry and apply Dimensional Magic. Punch holes through triangle and edge of card. Attach to card with tassel. Adhere frame and postage stamp to card. Use FabriTac to attach puddles of Itty Bitty Beads to centers of orchids.

Botanica Glove - MATERIALS: White matte glove card • Rubber stamps (Mini Moth, Orchid Expressions, Floral Textile) • Coal Ancient Page ink • VersaColor ink (Opera Pink, Pink, Orange) • Clear embossing powder • Multi Ultra Fine Crystal glitter • Postage stamp • Pink and Orange 24 gauge wire • Stipple brush • Heat tool • Round-nose pliers • Glue pen
TIP: Follow step by step instructions.

Congo Pin - MATERIALS: White Mini Matts • Rubber stamps (Royal Orchid Script, Congo Border) • Ink (Brown, Tan, Lime) • Deep Impression Clear embossing powder • Assorted beads • 24 gauge Green wire • 2 buttons • 1/8" hole punch • Round-nose pliers • Hot sheet • Craft pan • Metallic Gold marker • Colored pencils
TIPS: Punch holes in matts and stamp with Brown Royal Orchid Script and Congo Border. Color with inks. Place on Hot Sheet in pan heated to 300°F, sprinkle with Clear powder and melt. Attach mats with wire, buttons and beads. Adhere pin back.

Terrific Embellishment Ideas!

Leopard Orchid Card -
MATERIALS: White matte note card • Rubber stamps (Leopard Orchid, Cheetah Spots) • Pine Ancient Page ink • Ultra Fine Multi Crystal glitter • Button • Postage stamps • Flat glass marble • 1/4" Green sheer ribbon • 1/8" hole punch • Craft knife • Watercolor pencils • Glue pen • Glue

TIPS: Stamp designs on card with Pine ink. Color with pencils. Cut around bottom of one flower design. Collage with torn scraps of postage stamps. Adhere flat glass marble. Punch holes and attach button with ribbon bow.

1. Apply ink with stipple brush.

2. Stamp design all over card.

3. Stamp design, tear out and glue on card.

5. Adhere postage stamps.

6. Punch holes and add wire embellishments.

7. Add glue with glue pen and sprinkle with glitter.

Flocking

Go deep into the jungle and emerge with designs brimming with the romance of Africa!

1. Apply double-sided adhesive and stamp design with permanent ink. Cut away first area with craft knife.

2. For spots, peel off the protective film, and punch spots, replace film.

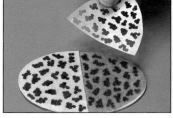

3. Apply first color of flock, remove protective film and apply second color.

Flocked Safari Frame - MATERIALS: Black Retro and Triangle Mini Matts • White craft frame • Rubber stamps (Zebra Stripes, Cheetah Spots, Primitive Fringe, Beaded Feather, African Mask, Orchid Elements) • Gold and White pigment inks • Black StazOn ink • White embossing powder • PEARLustre puddles • 22 gauge Gold wire • Assorted beads • Photo • Raffia • Peacock feather strips • 2 stamped feathers • Purple and Dark Green acrylic paints • Double-sided adhesive • Paintbrush • 1/16" and 1/8" hole punches • Craft knife • Heat tool • Feathers • FabriTac
TIPS: Trace frame on double-sided adhesive and cut out. Cut in sections and stamp designs with StazOn ink. Apply sections to frame and follow flocking instructions. Paint splotches on matts and let dry. Stamp Primitive Fringe and Orchid Elements on 2 matts with White ink and emboss with White. Melt puddles on other matts and stamp images with Gold ink. Punch holes and add wire and beads. Adhere all elements to frame. Insert photo and tie front and back of frames together with raffia, peacock strips and wire. Color pegs with ink, insert.

Feathered Female - MATERIALS: Black Millinery Mini Matts • Rubber stamps (Cheetah Spots, Stardust Points) • Clear embossing ink • Deep Impression Clear embossing powder • Gold embossing powder • Ivory paint • Feather • 24 gauge Russet wire • Assorted beads • Pin back • Chalk • 1/8" hole punch • Heat tool • Round-nose pliers • Metallic Copper marker • FabriTac • Terry cloth
TIPS: Stamp feather with Gold ink and emboss with Gold powder. Stamp Cheetah Spots on matt with Clear ink and emboss with Clear powder. Apply Ivory paint to matt and let dry. Use damp cloth to gently scrub paint from embossed areas. Rub with chalk. Punch holes and add wire and bead embellishments. Adhere feather and pin back.

Safari Necklace - MATERIALS: Tags (3 White matte, 3 Black glossy) • White cardstock • Rubber stamps (Snakeskin, Cheetah Spots, Prancing Zebra, Zebra Stripes, Palm Fronds, Tiger Pair, Leopard Texture Cube, Zig Zag Border) • Dye inks (Sienna, Pine, Mandarin, Black) • Clear ink • Embossing powders (Chinese Red, Silver, Copper) • Deep Impression Clear embossing powder • Black and White flock • Assorted 1/4" ribbon • Black cord • Assorted beads • 3 stamped feathers • Tassel cord • Yarn • Heat tool • 1/4" hole punch
TIPS: Stamp designs on White tags. Stipple color around edges. Stamp Snakeskin with Clear ink and emboss with Copper, Silver or Red on Black tags. Stamp Zebra stripes on cardstock with Clear ink and emboss with Clear powder before immediately adding Black or White flock. Cut out and punch holes. Attach all tags to Black cord. Tie ribbons, yarn tassel cord and add beads and stamped feathers between tags. Add beads to ends of necklace and knot.